C.A. Reilly
1959

Nuclear Magnetic Resonance

Nuclear Magnetic Resonance

APPLICATIONS TO ORGANIC CHEMISTRY

John D. Roberts

PROFESSOR OF ORGANIC CHEMISTRY
CALIFORNIA INSTITUTE OF TECHNOLOGY

McGRAW-HILL BOOK COMPANY, INC.

NEW YORK   TORONTO   LONDON   1959

Preface

This brief book is the outgrowth of some forty lectures in which it was attempted to explain the phenomenon of nuclear magnetic resonance absorption and the uses of high-resolution nuclear magnetic resonance spectroscopy to organic chemists whose background, like that of the author, has often been deficient in nuclear and electromagnetic theory. Quite a number of suggestions were received for presentation of the material in printed form with illustrations based on the lecture slides. This has now been done, and it is hoped that the result will be of service to practicing chemists and students as a guide to various applications of NMR spectroscopy and an introduction to more authoritative works. Throughout, the coverage is illustrative rather than comprehensive.

The author apologizes for choosing rather too many examples of applications from his own research, but it is always easiest to write about what one knows best. He is greatly indebted to Dr. W. D. Phillips of the E. I. du Pont Company for helping to kindle his interest in NMR research and to Dr. James N. Shoolery of Varian Associates and Professors V. Schomaker and H. M. McConnell for many patient hours of explanation with respect to both simple and difficult points of theory. The Office of Naval Research supported much of the research described herein which was carried out at the California Institute of Technology.

Dr. Shoolery kindly supplied material for several of the figures, and Dr. Marjorie C. Caserio helped greatly with many of the details in getting the book together. Helpful suggestions were received from Professors D. Y. Curtin, R. Breslow, and D. E. Applequist. Professors William S. Johnson and E. E. van Tamelen supplied several unpublished spectra for Chapters 2 and 3.

John D. Roberts

Contents

Preface . . . . **v**

1. Introduction. The Nuclear Resonance Phenomenon **1**

   1-1. Introduction 1
   1-2. Nuclear Magnetic Resonance Spectrometers 3
   1-3. Magnetic Properties of Nuclei. Nuclear Spin 5
   1-4. Magnetic Quantum Numbers 7
   1-5. Nuclear Precession 10
   1-6. Nuclear Relaxation 10
   1-7. Longitudinal Relaxation, T_1 12
   1-8. Transverse Relaxation, T_2 13
   1-9. The Nuclear Resonance Signal 14
  1-10. Relaxation Effects on NMR Signals 17
  1-11. Properties of Magnetic Nuclei of Interest to
       Organic Problems 18

2. The Chemical Shift **20**

   2-1. Introduction. The Chemical-shift Parameter 20
   2-2. Measurement of Chemical Shift 21
   2-3. Some Factors Which Influence δ 22
   2-4. Chemical Shifts for Other Nuclei 25
   2-5. Proton δ Values and Electronegativity 26
   2-6. δ and Hammett's σ Constants 27
   2-7. Resonance Signal Areas and Widths 30
   2-8. Chemical Shifts and Organic Structure Determinations.
       General Considerations 33
   2-9. Illustrative Analysis of a Reaction Product 40
  2-10. Accentuation of Chemical Shifts by Paramagnetic Salts . . 40

3. Spin-Spin Splitting **42**

3-1. The High-resolution Ethanol Spectrum   42
3-2. Spin-Spin Splitting in a Single Crystal   43
3-3. Spin-Spin Splitting in Liquids.   45
3-4. Spin-Spin Splitting in the Ethyl Group   46
3-5. More Complex Spin-Spin Splittings   48
3-6. Magnitudes of Coupling Constants   53
3-7. Coupling between Equivalent and Nearly Equivalent Protons .   55
3-8. Spin-Spin Couplings in Rigid Systems   57
3-9. Spin-Spin Splitting and Molecular Asymmetry   58

4. Nuclear Magnetic Resonance and Reaction Kinetics **61**

4-1. Introduction. Proton Exchange in Water–Acetic
     Acid Mixtures   61
4-2. Relationship between Resonance Line Shapes and
     Exchange Rates   63
4-3. Proton Exchange in Ethanol-Water Mixtures   64
4-4. Ethyl Acetoacetate and Its Enol Form   67
4-5. Rates of Rotation Around –CO–Nζ Bonds of Amides . . .   69
4-6. Restricted Rotation in Ethane Derivatives   71
4-7. Nitrogen Inversion Frequencies of Cyclic Imines   74
4-8. Proton Exchange in Ammonia and Ammonium Ions   . . .   76

5. Nuclear Quadrupole Relaxation Effects. Double Resonance . . .   **80**

5-1. Proton Resonance Line Broadening by ^{14}N   80
5-2. Nuclear Quadrupoles and Quadrupole-induced Relaxation . .   81
5-3. Proton N–H Resonance of Pyrrole. Double Resonance   . .   83
5-4. Quadrupole-induced Relaxation with Other Nuclei   84
5-5. Applications of Double Resonance   86

Appendix A. The Bloch Equations **88**

Appendix B.   Bibliography **99**

Appendix C. Problems **100**

Name Index **111**

Subject Index **113**

Nuclear Magnetic Resonance

CHAPTER 1

Introduction. The Nuclear Resonance Phenomenon

1-1. Introduction

The development of nuclear magnetic resonance spectroscopy subsequent to the initial discoveries by Purcell [1] and Bloch [2] in 1946 is now recognized as one of the most important events in the last fifty years for the advancement of organic chemistry. Nuclear magnetic resonance (NMR) techniques are throwing new light on many difficult organic problems. With the possible exception of gas-liquid chromatography, no new experimental method has been so rapidly accepted or proved so widely applicable. It is the purpose of this book to present the elements of NMR spectroscopy in a form suitable for practical use by organic chemists. Examples of applications will be mainly drawn from high-resolution proton resonance spectroscopy, but the principles so illustrated will often be useful in dealing with other types of NMR spectroscopy.

An NMR spectrometer consists basically of a magnet, radio-frequency (rf) transmitter or oscillator, and a suitable rf detector. When a sample of a material comprised of atoms having nuclei with certain magnetic properties (to be described later) is placed in the magnet pole gap and subjected to the rf field of the oscillator, absorption of rf energy (resonance) occurs at particular combinations of the oscillator frequency and the magnetic field strength and an rf signal is picked up by the detector. Customarily, the detector output is measured at constant oscillator frequency as a function of the magnetic field strength, although there

[1] E. M. Purcell, H. C. Torrey, and R. V. Pound, *Phys. Rev.,* **69,** 37 (1946).
[2] F. Bloch, W. W. Hansen, and M. E. Packard, *Phys. Rev.,* **69,** 127 (1946).

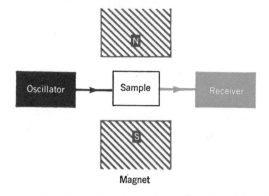

Magnet

are advantages to the alternative procedure of maintaining the magnetic field constant and varying the oscillator frequency.[3]

Information of chemical interest arises from the fact that nuclei of atoms in different chemical environments are also generally in quite different magnetic environments and come into resonance with a fixed-frequency oscillator at different values of the applied magnetic field. Figure 1-1 shows a nuclear magnetic resonance spectrogram of a typical organic molecule, N-ethylethylenimine.

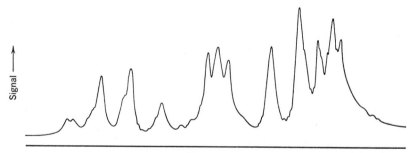

Fig. 1-1. Proton NMR spectrum of N-ethylethylenimine at an oscillator frequency of 40 Mc and a magnetic field of 9,400 gauss.

Besides the obvious utility of such a spectrogram to serve as a finger-print of the compound in question, much more information can be gleaned from the spectrum than is provided by a qualitative examination of its major features. For example, it can be stated with a high degree of certainty that an ethyl group is present and also that the methyl of the ethyl group is rotating about the bond connecting it to the methylene considerably more than 15 times per second. In addition, the spectrum

[3] E. B. Baker and L. W. Burd, *Rev. Sci. Instr.*, **28**, 313 (1957).

shows the imine nitrogen to have a configuration such that the nitrogen atom and the three carbon atoms to which it is directly attached do not lie in a plane. Furthermore, we can say that the nitrogen atom is not undergoing configurational inversion of the kind shown in the following equation at a rate approaching or greater than 80 times per second.

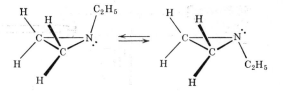

Clearly, the NMR spectrum of the compound is a veritable treasure trove of useful information not easily obtainable in any other way.

We shall now consider the connection between the structure of an organic molecule and its NMR spectrum with the intention of ultimately getting at the principles which enable one to derive the kind of inferences made above. At the outset, we shall show how magnetic nuclei can absorb rf energy and produce an rf signal in the detector. Only the "crossed-coil" nuclear induction apparatus developed by Bloch, Hansen, and Packard [2] will be considered, since it provides the basis for the commercially available high-resolution spectrometers.

1-2.   Nuclear Magnetic Resonance Spectrometers

A block diagram of an NMR spectrometer utilizing an electromagnet is shown in Fig. 1-2. For high-resolution spectra, the magnet will have pole faces up to 12 in. in diameter, a pole gap of about 1.75 in., and a field of up to 14,000 gauss. The magnet is energized by a highly stable d-c power supply. If a fixed-frequency rf oscillator is employed, one "sweeps" through the resonance by varying the total magnetic field through injection of the linearly varying output from a "sweep generator" into coils either wound around the magnet pole faces or located within the pole gap. The output of the generator is synchronized with the trace along the X axis of an oscilloscope or suitable graphic recorder.

The sample is placed within the pole gap and subjected to the rf alternating magnetic field produced by passing a high-frequency a-c current through the oscillator coil. The detector serves to pick up changes in the magnetization of the nuclei induced by the rf oscillator, and the detector signal is fed to the Y axis of the oscilloscope or graphic recorder. A nuclear resonance spectrogram is thus a plot of detector signal against magnetic field at constant oscillator frequency.

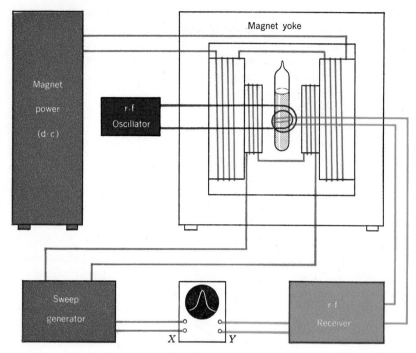

Fig. 1-2. A block diagram showing NMR spectrometer equipped with an electro-magnet.

The state of affairs in the immediate vicinity of the sample is shown in Fig. 1-3. It will be seen that the oscillator coil is oriented with its axis perpendicular to the principal magnetic field. The receiver coil is tuned to the oscillator frequency but is oriented with its axis perpendicular to both the direction of the principal magnetic field and the axis of the oscillator coil. This arrangement is used to minimize the overloading of the necessarily sensitive receiver which would result from direct coupling between the oscillator and receiver coils. Therefore, a nuclear resonance signal arises from an indirect coupling between the oscillator and receiver coils produced by the sample itself. The requirements for such coupling can be described more precisely as follows. The magnetic field of the oscillator alternates through the sample along one direction. The receiver coil responds to a magnetic field which alternates perpendicularly to the field produced by the oscillator coil. The signal results from an alternating magnetization which is induced in the sample by the oscillator field in a direction perpendicular to the axis of the oscillator coil.

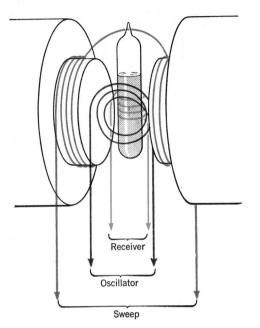

Fig. 1-3. Arrangement of sample and coils in nuclear induction apparatus.

1-3. Magnetic Properties of Nuclei. Nuclear Spin

Induction of an alternating magnetization in a substance like an organic compound, by an oscillatory magnetic field as described above, can be shown by isotopic substitution procedures to involve certain types of atomic nuclei which act like tiny magnets. In the ensuing discussion of magnetic properties of nuclei, we shall find it convenient to ascribe certain electromechanical properties to nuclei which are gross oversimplifications of the real state of affairs but are nonetheless very helpful in explaining how a nuclear resonance signal can arise.

In some ways, certain nuclei behave as though they are nonspinning spherical bodies with the nuclear charge distributed evenly over their surfaces. This type of nucleus does not have a magnetic moment because there is no circulation of the nuclear charge. We also say that the "nuclear quadrupole moment" is zero because, when a probing electrical charge approaches such a nucleus, it experiences an electrostatic field, the magnitude of which is independent of the direction of approach. These nuclei are said to have their "nuclear spin" value equal to zero and, not having a magnetic moment, they can give no nuclear resonance signal. Many nuclei of considerable importance to organic

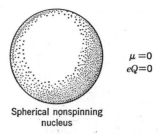

$\mu = 0$
$eQ = 0$

Spherical nonspinning
nucleus

chemistry, particularly ^{12}C and ^{16}O, are of this type as, in fact, are all nuclei whose mass numbers A and charges Z are both even.

It is not so unfortunate as it might seem that the principal isotope of carbon can give no nuclear magnetic resonance signal, since if ^{12}C had a sizable nuclear moment the proton NMR spectra of most organic compounds would be much more complicated than they actually are. Furthermore, ^{13}C has a magnetic moment so that when there is vital necessity for observing a carbon resonance signal, ^{13}C can usually be used, either at its prevailing low natural concentration or with the aid of ^{13}C-enriched material.

A number of nuclei of particular importance to organic chemistry may be assigned nuclear spin values of $\frac{1}{2}$. This means that they act as though they were spherical bodies possessing uniform charge distributions but spinning like tops. A spinning nucleus has circulating charge, and this generates a magnetic field so that a nuclear magnetic moment results. The spherical charge distribution ascribed to nuclei with spin of $\frac{1}{2}$ means that a probing charge approaching them experiences the same electrostatic field regardless of the direction of approach and, therefore, as with the spherical nonspinning nuclei, the electric quadrupole moment is zero. Nuclei with a spin of $\frac{1}{2}$ include ^{1}H, ^{13}C, ^{15}N,

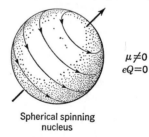

$\mu \neq 0$
$eQ = 0$

Spherical spinning
nucleus

^{19}F, and ^{31}P, and, in general, such nuclei are particularly favorable for nuclear resonance experiments.

A very large number of magnetic nuclei act as though they are spinning bodies with nonspherical charge distributions and are assigned spin values of unity or larger integral multiples of $\frac{1}{2}$. Often such nuclei are taken to approximate ellipsoids spinning about the principal axis. A charged, elongated (prolate) ellipsoid with the charge uniformly distributed over its surface will present an anisotropic electrostatic field to an approaching unit charge so that the electrostatic work will be different in bringing up a unit charge to a given distance if the charge approaches along the spin axis or at some angle to it. By convention, the electric quadrupole moment of a nucleus ascribed the shape of a prolate ellipsoid is assigned a value greater than zero. Important examples are ^{2}H and ^{14}N.

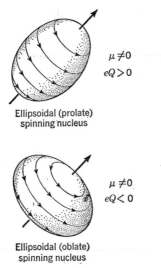

$\mu \neq 0$
$eQ > 0$

Ellipsoidal (prolate)
spinning nucleus

$\mu \neq 0$
$eQ < 0$

Ellipsoidal (oblate)
spinning nucleus

Nuclei which behave like charged, flattened (oblate) ellipsoids also present an anisotropic electric field to a probing charge and by convention are assigned negative electric-quadrupole-moment values. Nuclei of this type include ^{17}O, ^{33}S, ^{35}Cl, etc. In the ensuing discussion, we shall confine our attention largely to nuclei with a spin of $\frac{1}{2}$, since, as will be seen, complications are often introduced when the electric quadrupole moment is different from zero. These complications are in themselves capable of providing useful chemical information but are not helpful to an understanding of the operation of a nuclear resonance spectrometer.

1-4. Magnetic Quantum Numbers

An important property of spinning nuclei is that their magnetic moment vectors appear to have only certain specified average values in any given direction, such as along the axis of the principal magnetic field. The permitted values of the vector moment along the direction of interest can be described with the aid of a set of magnetic quantum numbers m, which are derivable from the nuclear spin I and the relation $m = I, (I-1)(I-2), \ldots, -I$. Thus, if I is $\frac{1}{2}$, the possible magnetic quantum numbers are $+\frac{1}{2}$ and $-\frac{1}{2}$, and if the magnetic moment is μ, the possible values of the vector components of the moment in the direction of the principal magnetic field H will be $+\mu_H$ and $-\mu_H$, as shown below. If I is unity, then the possible magnetic quantum num-

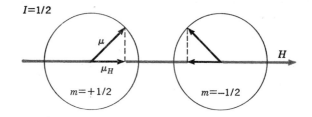

bers are $+1$, 0, and -1, and the vector along the field direction will have possible values corresponding to the nucleus being oriented so as to have a component in the same direction as the field vector, perpendicular to the field vector, or opposite in direction to the field vector.

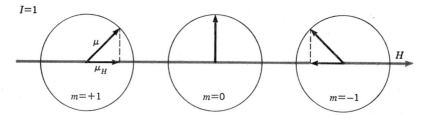

In the absence of a magnetic field there will be no preference for one or the other of the two possible magnetic quantum numbers for a nucleus with I equal to $\frac{1}{2}$. In a large assemblage of such nuclei, there will be then exactly equal numbers with m equal to $+\frac{1}{2}$ and m equal to $-\frac{1}{2}$. In a magnetic field, the nuclei will tend to assume the magnetic quantum number $(+\frac{1}{2})$ which represents alignment with the field in just the same way as compass needles tend to line up in the earth's magnetic field. Thus, in the presence of a magnetic field, $m = +\frac{1}{2}$ represents a more favorable energy state than $m = -\frac{1}{2}$ [provided the gyromagnetic ratio γ (see Sec. 1-5) is positive]. However, the tendency of the nuclei to assume the magnetic quantum number $+\frac{1}{2}$ is opposed by thermal agitation. The nuclear moment, field strength, and temperature can be used to calculate the equilibrium percentages of the nuclei in each quantum state by the Boltzmann distribution law. At room temperature, even in rather high magnetic fields such as 10,000 gauss, thermal agitation is so important relative to the energy gained by alignment of the nuclei that only a very slight excess of the nuclei go into the more favorable quantum state, as shown by the following:

$$N = Ap \exp\left(-\frac{\varepsilon}{kT}\right) \qquad \text{(Boltzmann equation)}$$

$$\varepsilon = -\mu_H H = -\frac{\gamma h}{2\pi} mH$$

For protons at 300°K in a field of 9,400 gauss

$$\frac{N(+\frac{1}{2})}{N(-\frac{1}{2})} = \exp\left(\frac{\gamma hH/2\pi}{kT}\right) = 1.0000066$$

This situation is analogous to an assemblage of compasses on a table subjected to violent agitation. The movements of the table tend to throw the compass needles out of alignment with the earth's magnetic field, so that on the average only a very slight excess of the needles may be actually pointing north.

Nuclear magnetic resonance spectroscopy is primarily concerned with transitions of the nuclei in a magnetic field between energy levels which are expressed by the different magnetic quantum numbers. These energy changes are analogous to electronic and vibrational-rotational energy changes in other forms of spectroscopy. There is no direct magnetic interaction between the nuclei and the electrons which surround them. Thus, a problem is posed with regard to the transfer of energy from the nuclei to and from their surroundings. The energy-transfer problem may be restated in the following way. Consider an assemblage of nuclei in the absence of a magnetic field. As stated before, there will be exactly equal numbers of nuclei with the magnetic quantum numbers $+\frac{1}{2}$ and $-\frac{1}{2}$. In the presence of a magnetic field, this distribution corresponds to an infinitely high temperature because the state with the magnetic quantum number $-\frac{1}{2}$ is now energetically less favorable than the $+\frac{1}{2}$ state and only an infinitely high temperature could produce sufficient thermal agitation to keep the nuclear magnets from having some net alignment in the field direction. In order to achieve the equilibrium distribution of nuclei between the two possible spin states at a lower temperature, it is necessary that energy be lost to the surroundings by nuclear "relaxation." Relaxation is hardly expected to be a simple process, since the nuclei are not easily able to collide with one another or the surrounding electrons and convert their energy due to an external magnetic field into molecular vibrational, rotational, or translational energy. Transfer of energy back and forth among nuclei in various magnetic quantum states and their surroundings can be achieved with the aid of another property which might be ascribed to magnetic nuclei, called "nuclear precession."

1-5.   Nuclear Precession

When a nucleus with a magnetic moment is placed in a magnetic field, it acts as though it were undergoing precession around the field axis at an angular velocity ω_0, which is directly proportional to the magnetic field at the nucleus H_0. This precession is analogous to the precession

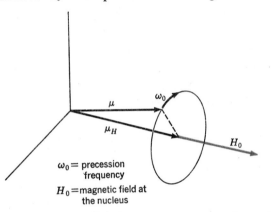

$\omega_0 =$ precession frequency

$H_0 =$ magnetic field at the nucleus

of a spinning gyroscope when allowed to topple in the earth's gravitational field. The direction of precession of a gyroscope depends on the direction of its angular momentum vector, and the angular velocity depends on the magnitude of the angular momentum vector and the strength of the gravitational field to which it is subjected. For nuclei, the proportionality constant γ between the angular velocity of precession and the field strength depends on the angular spin momentum and the magnetic moment of the nucleus. γ is called the "gyromagnetic" ratio or, less commonly, the "magnetogyric" ratio. All nuclei of the same charge and mass number have the same gyromagnetic ratio. Thus, all protons act as though they precess at the same angular velocity when the magnetic field strength *at the nucleus* is the same. γ may be either positive or negative, corresponding to different directions of precession.

1-6.   Nuclear Relaxation

The property of magnetic nuclei which corresponds to precession

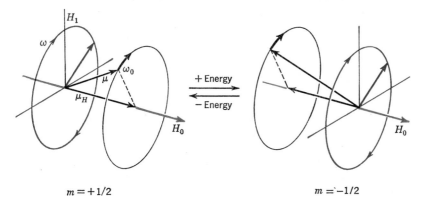

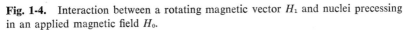

$$m = +1/2 \qquad\qquad m = -1/2$$

Fig. 1-4. Interaction between a rotating magnetic vector H_1 and nuclei precessing in an applied magnetic field H_0.

provides a means whereby energy may be transferred back and forth between the nuclei and their surroundings. Consider a magnetic field vector arranged so as to rotate perpendicular to a magnetic field in which are immersed magnetic nuclei precessing at the angular velocity ω_0 (Fig. 1-4). If the rotating vector has a quite different angular velocity from the precessing nuclei, the rotating field vector and the precessing nuclear magnetic vectors cannot remain in phase and there will be no effective interaction between them. On the other hand, if the rotating field vector has the same angular velocity as the precessing nuclear vectors, it will remain in phase with them and can exert a magnetic torque tending to flip over the orientation of the nuclei and thence change their magnetic quantum numbers. Of course, if the nuclear magnetic quantum numbers change, energy is transferred to or from the agency producing the rotating field vector. Thus, an assemblage of nuclear magnets immersed in a magnetic field can come to thermal equilibrium with its surroundings.

An important mechanism for relaxation of a group of nuclei at a nonequilibrium spin temperature utilizes atomic and molecular thermal motions as follows. Suppose a magnetic nucleus is surrounded by others of its type contained in atoms undergoing violent thermal motions. The thermal motions of the nuclei produce random oscillatory magnetic fields which can have frequency components with frequencies equal to the precession frequencies of the relaxing nuclei and can act as a rotating magnetic field vector so as to permit the magnetic orientation energy to be converted to thermal energy. The rate of relaxation by this mechanism depends on the temperature, the concentration of magnetic nuclei, and the viscosity of the medium. It is kinetically a first-order process and can be expressed in terms of a "relaxation time," which is the mean lifetime of the excess of nuclei in the nonrelaxed state. Thermal relaxation is often slow, on the order of seconds to weeks. A vivid example is provided by ^{13}C of natural abundance located at the central atom of neopentane molecules. The natural abundance of ^{13}C is so low that such atoms will usually be connected only to nonmagnetic ^{12}C atoms and thus are sterically shielded from other magnetic nuclei such as the methyl protons in the same or surrounding molecules. As a result, the rotating field components produced by the thermal motions of the surrounding magnetic nuclei are not very effective at aiding the relaxation of the central ^{13}C nucleus, and the mean lifetime before relaxation is very long.

As might be expected, thermal motions of substances with unpaired electrons are particularly effective in inducing thermal relaxation, and such paramagnetic substances present as impurities may spoil high-resolution spectra by making the relaxation times very short, which, as will be seen later, results in line-broadening.

In summary, transitions between states with various magnetic quantum numbers which have different energies because of an applied magnetic field may be induced by thermal motions of magnetic nuclei or paramagnetic substances or else by an external rotating magnetic field which has a frequency equal or very nearly equal to the precession frequency of the nuclei.

1-7. Longitudinal Relaxation, T_1

It turns out that there are two varieties of relaxation. The first, discussed above, has to do with the establishment of thermal equilibrium between an assemblage of nuclear magnets with different quantum numbers. This is "longitudinal" relaxation, since it results in establishment of an equilibrium value of the nuclear magnetization along the magnetic field axis. Thus, an assemblage of nuclei in a very weak magnetic field, such as the earth's magnetic field, will have essentially no net magnetization of the nuclei along the field axis, since only a few more of the nuclei possess the spin quantum number $+\frac{1}{2}$ as compared with those with the value of $-\frac{1}{2}$. When this assemblage is placed in a magnetic field and relaxation takes place, there is an increase in the sample magnetization along the field axis as more of the nuclei drop into the lower energy state with magnetic quantum number of $+\frac{1}{2}$. The characteristic longitudinal relaxation time is designated as T_1.

1-8.   Transverse Relaxation, T_2

The other variety of relaxation may be illustrated as follows. Consider a group of nuclei which are precessing in phase about the axis of a common magnetic field. If the nuclei were all centered on the same point, their magnetic vectors would be precessing together like a tied-up bundle of sticks. If we take the magnetic field axis to be the Z axis, the nuclei precessing in phase produce a resultant rotating magnetic

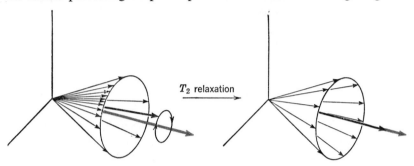

T_2 relaxation

vector which has a component in the XY plane. If by any process the nuclei tend to lose their phase coherence, their resultant will move toward the Z axis and the macroscopic component of magnetization in the XY plane will go to zero. This type of relaxation is commonly referred to as "transverse" relaxation, and its rate is customarily expressed in terms of the characteristic time T_2. Characteristic time T_2 is the time constant for the kinetically first-order decay of X, Y magnetization.

There are several factors which can contribute to transverse relaxation, and these may be classified as intrinsic in the nature of the sample or arising from the equipment used. The homogeneity of the applied magnetic field will be extremely important as an external factor. If the assemblage of nuclei under consideration is in a nonhomogeneous field, the nuclei will not have identical precession frequencies, and if they start off in phase, they will soon get out of phase because of their different precession rates. In many cases, the inhomogeneity of the applied magnetic field will be the most important factor determining T_2. Nonhomogeneous magnetic fields within the sample will also decrease T_2. Viscosity plays an important part here. In the liquid state, nuclei which might otherwise be expected to have the same precession frequency will not usually have instantaneously identical environments as regards nuclear magnetic dipole-dipole interaction and diamagnetic shielding involving neighboring molecules. Thus, the nucleus of one atom may have one type of molecule as a neighbor while another nucleus may have quite a different molecule as a neighbor. Such nuclei will in general be subjected to different magnetic fields and have different precession frequencies, thus permitting them to lose phase coherence. This effect will be of most importance in viscous media where the molecules move slowly with respect to one another. If the viscosity is low and the molecules tumble rapidly relative to the precession frequencies of their nuclei, the fluctuations in the local magnetic fields are effectively averaged to zero and T_2 is thereby increased.

Another factor which influences T_2 in solids or viscous liquids is the occurrence of what are often called "spin-spin collisions." These "collisions" occur when two identical nuclei exchange spins—one nucleus acting as a rotating field vector for the other. It can be shown by the uncertainty principle that spin-spin collisions limit the time of maintenance of phase coherence for an assemblage of identical nuclei precessing in phase and thus decrease T_2. As will be seen, both T_1 and T_2 are vitally important in determining the character of nuclear resonance signals.

1-9. The Nuclear Resonance Signal

The operation of the nuclear magnetic resonance spectrometer may now be discussed in terms of the magnetic properties of nuclei outlined

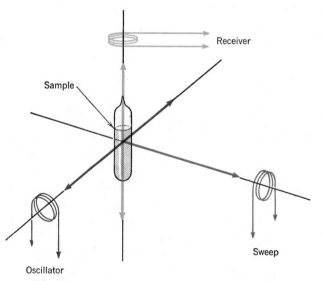

Fig. 1-5. Magnetic forces operating on sample in an NMR spectrometer.

above. As a quick review, we note as before that the sample is subjected to (1) a large magnetic field varied by the sweep generator and
directed along the Z axis and (2) an alternating magnetic field along
the X axis produced by the oscillator coil (Fig. 1-5). The receiver coil
is oriented so as to respond to an alternating magnetic field along the
Y axis, and the oscillator must induce a component of Y magnetization
in the sample if a signal is to be picked up by the receiver. At the
nuclear level, the situation is as shown in Fig. 1-6. In the first place,
we note that an assemblage of magnetic nuclei placed in a magnetic
field undergo relaxation and reach an equilibrium distribution in which
there is a slight excess with the magnetic quantum number $+\frac{1}{2}$. This
excess of nuclei with $m = +\frac{1}{2}$ combine to give a small macroscopic
resultant magnetization in the Z direction. In addition, each nucleus
acts as if it were precessing around the magnetic field axis with the
angular velocity ω_0 (equal to γH_0). At the beginning of a nuclear
magnetic resonance experiment, the nuclei will have no phase coherence
and the excess of nuclear magnets with $m = +\frac{1}{2}$ is represented graph-
ically by having the individual magnetic vectors distributed evenly over
the surface of a cone whose axis coincides with the direction of the
magnetic field. In this situation, there will be no net X, Y component
of nuclear magnetization.

Consider the nuclei to be now subjected to an alternating magnetic
field in the X direction produced by the rf oscillator. This field will
have no net component in the Y direction, but we can consider that
it is made up of two equal magnetic vectors rotating at the same velocity

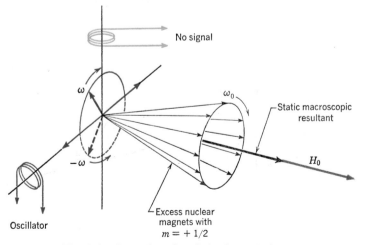

Fig. 1-6.   Start of nuclear induction experiment.

in opposite directions with phase relations so that they exactly cancel each other in the Y direction. One of these vectors will be rotating in the same direction as the nuclear magnets precess while the other will be rotating in the opposite direction. Of course, the field which is rotating oppositely to the direction of nuclear precession will not interact with the nuclei because it cannot stay in phase with them. However, the field which is rotating in the same direction can stay in phase with and tend to flip over the nuclear magnets, provided it has the same angular velocity (see Sec. 1-6).

In a typical nuclear magnetic resonance experiment, we change the precession frequency of the nuclei by varying the applied magnetic field and keep the oscillator frequency constant. At some value of the field, the nuclear precession frequency becomes equal to the frequency of the rotating field vector produced by the oscillator, and energy may then be transferred from the oscillator to the nuclei, causing some of them to go to the higher energy state with $m = -\frac{1}{2}$. At the same time, the rotating field vector acts to tip the vectors of the individual nuclear magnets, with which it is 90° out of phase, away from the field axis and thus causes the axis of the cone of vectors to "wobble" around the field axis at the precession frequency. This has an effect such as would result from bunching the nuclear vectors as shown in Fig. 1-7, so that the macroscopic resultant is moved away from the field axis and produces a rotating component of magnetization in the X and Y directions which, of course, precesses around the field axis with the same angular velocity as the individual nuclei. This alternating field in the Y direction induces a current in the receiver coil and thus generates an NMR signal.

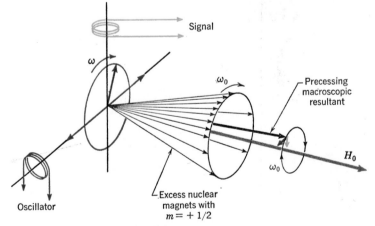

Fig. 1-7.   Conditions at resonance $\omega_0 \cong \omega$.

As the magnetic field is increased through action of the sweep generator, the nuclei increase their precession frequencies and drop out of phase with the rotating field vector. At this point, transverse and longitudinal relaxation return the nuclear magnetization of the nuclei in the X, Y, and Z directions to the equilibrium values. As the Y magnetization decreases by transverse relaxation, the signal dies away in the receiver.

1-10. Relaxation Effects on NMR Signals

It should be emphasized that relaxation begins as soon as the nuclei absorb energy from the rotating field vector. Obviously, if T_1 and T_2 are both extremely short, the signal strength at a given field value will be very small because both longitudinal and transverse relaxation destroy the component of magnetization in the X, Y directions. On the other hand, if the relaxation times are long, other effects are noted. For example, if T_1 is very long, a "saturation" effect may be noted with respect to the signal strength because the energy absorbed by the nuclei from the oscillator is not readily dissipated to the surroundings. In this situation, the nuclei reach an equilibrium distribution between their magnetic quantum states which is determined by the relaxation time T_1. When T_1 is short, the nuclei remain more or less at thermal equilibrium with their surroundings and the absorption of energy then depends primarily on T_2.

It should be clear that if one were suddenly to turn off the oscillator in the middle of a resonance signal, the signal would not cease at once because the rate of loss of magnetization in the X, Y directions depends on both T_1 and T_2. This sort of effect leads to pronounced differences in the appearance of NMR signals, depending on the rate of sweep, as illustrated in Fig. 1-8. A fast sweep produces a signal peak followed by a succession of diminishing peaks, which are often called "relaxation wiggles." A slow sweep gives a more symmetrical peak with perhaps

Fast sweep   Slow sweep

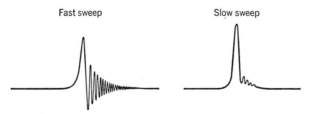

Fig. 1-8. Relaxation effects in fast and slow sweeps through the benzene resonance. Fast sweep displays "relaxation wiggles."

only a trace of the relaxation wiggles. The "envelope" of relaxation wiggles arises in the following way. The first peak of a plot of signal vs. magnetic field represents the point at which the precession frequency of the nuclei is equal to the oscillator frequency. As the field sweep continues from this point, the precession frequency increases and, hence, the precessing macroscopic resultant goes out of phase with the oscillator while the X, Y magnetization diminishes by longitudinal and transverse relaxation. Whenever the precessing macroscopic vector gains 360° on the rotating field vector, it comes into phase again with that vector and picks up an increment of X, Y magnetization which produces an increase in the signal strength. Repetitions of this process give a series of signal pulsations which finally cease when transverse relaxation is complete. Obviously, the slope of the decay envelope of the relaxation wiggles is a measure of T_2. It has been shown by comparison of the decay envelopes of their relaxation wiggles [4] that hydrogens in different chemical environments (as the methyl and phenyl groups of toluene) have quite different T_2 values.

1-11.   Properties of Magnetic Nuclei of Interest to Organic Problems

Table 1–1 shows some of the magnetic properties of nuclei of particular interest to organic chemists. The comparison of relative sensitivities to detection of NMR signals for different nuclei is of particular importance. These sensitivities are computed for equal numbers of nuclei at a constant field strength, which normally is taken as high as practically possible within limitations of field homogeneity, stability, etc. The sensitivity figure given for deuterons must be corrected for their low natural abundance in order to have a measure of the relative ease of detecting deuterium NMR signals in material containing the natural proportions of the hydrogen isotopes. It is seen that protons and ^{19}F are particularly favorable nuclei for observation. The precession frequencies of the nuclei are expressed in Table 1–1 in units of megacycles per 10,000 gauss and are seen to cover a very wide range of values. For high-resolution NMR spectroscopy, the rf oscillator must be extremely stable because oscillator stability is just as important to good resolution as is the homogeneity and stability of the magnetic field. As it is difficult to make a highly stable oscillator with a continuously variable frequency, customarily one uses separate fixed frequency units set at 3, 10, 20, 30, 40, and 60 Mc. The magnetic field is then ad-

---

[4] G. W. Nederbrogt and C. A. Reilly, *J. Chem. Phys.,* **24**, 1110 (1956); C. A. Reilly and R. L. Strombotne, *J. Chem. Phys.,* **26**, 1338 (1957).

Table 1–1. Magnetic Properties of Representative Nuclei

Nucleus	Z	I	Mc/kgauss	% Natural abundance	Relative sensitivity*
^{1}H	1	1/2	42.6	99.98	1.000
^{2}H	1	1	6.5	0.016	0.0096
^{13}C	6	1/2	10.7	1.11	0.016
^{14}N	7	1	3.1	99.63	0.0010
^{15}N	7	1/2	−4.3	0.37	0.0010
^{17}O	8	5/2	−5.8	0.04	0.029
^{19}F	9	1/2	40.1	100	0.834
^{31}P	15	1/2	17.2	100	0.066

* For equal numbers of nuclei at constant field.

justed to bring the nuclear precession frequencies to the appropriate oscillator frequency. In this way, one can cover a wide range of nuclei, keeping the magnetic field between 5,000 and 14,000 gauss. In general, the oscillator frequency is chosen which corresponds to the highest possible value of the field consistent with good homogeneity and stability because the sensitivity increases with field strength as does the separation between resonance lines corresponding to nuclei in different chemical environments.

A more mathematical treatment of nuclear resonance absorption is presented in Appendix A for the purpose of elucidating the differences between the absorption and dispersion modes and the nature of certain probe adjustments which may influence the shapes of resonance signal curves.

CHAPTER 2

The Chemical Shift

2-1.   Introduction.   The Chemical-shift Parameter

A low-resolution proton NMR spectrum of ethyl alcohol at a field of 9,400 gauss and an oscillator frequency of 40 Mc is shown in Fig. 2-1. The three resonance lines correspond to protons with different precession frequencies, which come into resonance with the oscillator frequency at different values of the magnetic field. The areas under the peaks stand roughly in the ratio 1:2:3, as would be expected if each peak corresponded to the chemically different OH, CH_2, and CH_3 ethanol protons. These assignments have been substantiated by studies of other alcohols and substitution of deuterium for hydrogen. Thus, if the hydroxyl proton of ethyl alcohol is replaced by deuterium, the resonance peak on the left disappears. To be sure, deuterium can give a nuclear resonance signal, but reference to Table 1–1 shows that its resonance frequency would be 6.1 Mc at 9,400 gauss. Therefore, with

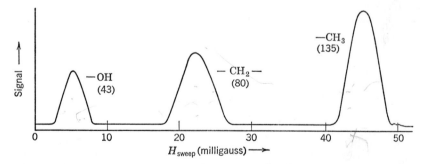

Fig. 2-1. Low-resolution NMR spectogram of ethanol protons at 40 Mc and 9,400 gauss. Numbers in parentheses adjacent to each peak are experimental figures for peak areas in arbitrary units.

20

a 40-Mc oscillator, the deuterium resonance would not be observed until the magnetic field reached 58,000 gauss, which is 10^6 times the total sweep shown in Fig. 2-1.

The spacing between the ethanol absorption lines is found to be directly proportional to the magnetic field, and if one operates at an oscillator frequency of 30 Mc and a field of 7,000 gauss, the resonance lines are three-fourths as far apart. Field-dependent differences between resonance line positions are called "chemical shifts" and arise because the lines of force of the applied magnetic field tend to be turned away from the nuclei by a diamagnetic shielding effect (but can also be turned in by a second-order paramagnetic effect) of the surrounding electrons. The degree of diamagnetic shielding is directly proportional to the applied field, and therefore chemical shifts are directly proportional to the magnetic field. In order that workers with NMR equipment having different oscillator frequencies and magnetic fields may have a simple basis for comparison of spectra, it is common to report resonance line positions in terms of a dimensionless parameter δ, which is the proportionality constant between resonance frequency and field strength. Usually, δ is expressed relative to some standard substance— for protons customarily water, benzene, or cyclohexane, each of which has only a single resonance line.

$$\delta = \frac{H_{sample} - H_{reference}}{H_{reference}} \times 10^6$$

2-2.   Measurement of Chemical Shift

Chemical shifts can be measured in several ways. It is quite simple to use an internal standard such as is provided by a sharp resonance line from a solvent or added solute. However, a number of investigations have indicated that internal standards must be used with some care because of possible specific solvent effects and the like. In the final analysis, the best comparisons will be of chemical shifts determined as a function of concentration in a given solvent and extrapolated to infinite dilution. However, this procedure is time consuming, particularly since there is no one solvent which is useful for all types of organic molecules. The special advantage of internal standards as an aid to rapid qualitative analysis of functional groups will be discussed later.

Chemical shifts can be conveniently measured relative to an external standard by using a set of concentric tubes, the standard occupying one compartment and the substance under investigation the other. The separation between the standard and sample resonance lines can be taken directly off the recorder chart if the magnetic field sweep is highly stable and linear. Such conditions are not often met in practice and it

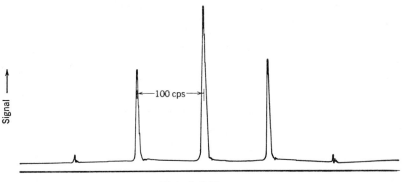

Fig. 2-2. Proton resonance spectrum of benzene at 40 Mc with 100-cps audio frequency superimposed.

is common to measure line separations by the audio-oscillator beat method.[1] To do this, one superimposes an audio frequency on the oscillator output, so that the sample is subjected to rotating magnetic field vectors corresponding not only to the principal frequency but also to the beat frequencies which are equal to the principal frequency plus or minus integral multiples of the audio frequency. If the audio power is suitably adjusted, the spectrum of a substance with a single resonance line like benzene appears as shown in Fig. 2-2, with the superimposed audio frequency at 100 cps. The positions of the so-called "sidebands" on the principal resonance can be varied by adjustment of the audio frequency so as to coincide with other signals whose positions are to be measured. With a reasonably stable oscillator, line positions can be determined by this method to better than ±1 cps. For crude measurements of line positions, it often suffices to use a substitution method in which the sweep rate is fixed, and when the desired resonance is observed, the sample is quickly removed and a standard is inserted with a resonance which falls fairly close to the one that is to be measured.

2-3.   Some Factors Which Influence δ

In general, the chemical shift parameter δ will be a function of the electron density around the nucleus, since the electrons are directly involved in the diamagnetic shielding which acts to attenuate the applied magnetic field. Specific solvent and bulk diamagnetic susceptibility effects will also be important in determining δ. Temperature is not

[1] J. T. Arnold and M. E. Packard, *J. Chem. Phys.,* **19,** 1608 (1951).

Table 2–1.   Typical Proton δ Values ($\times 10^6$) for Pure Liquids with Approximate Variations for Different Compounds *

–SO₃H	−6.7 ± 0.3	H₂O	(0.00)
–CO₂H	−6.4 ± 0.8	–OCH₃	+1.6 ± 0.3
RCHO	−4.7 ± 0.3	–CH₂X	+1.7 ± 1.2
RCONH₂	−2.9	≡C–H	+2.4 ± 0.4
ArOH	−2.3 ± 0.3	=C̣–CH₃	+3.3 ± 0.5
ArH	−1.9 ± 1.0	–CH₂–	+3.5 ± 0.5
=CH₂	−0.6 ± 0.7	RNH₂	+3.6 ± 0.7
ROH	−0.1 ± 0.7	–C̣–CH₃	+4.1 ± 0.6

* Data from L. H. Meyer, A. Saika, and H. S. Gutowsky, *J. Am. Chem. Soc.,* **75,** 4567 (1953).

usually very important unless a change in temperature causes marked changes in some type of association equilibrium. For example, the O–H resonance line of ethanol moves toward the CH₂ and CH₃ lines with increasing temperature probably because of changes in the concentrations of the various hydrogen-bonded species.[1] A similar effect is noted when ethanol is diluted with carbon tetrachloride.[2] At low concentrations, the O–H absorption appears between that of the methylene and methyl groups. Extrapolation of the position of the O–H line as a function of concentration to infinite dilution indicates that in such circumstances the O–H line would be at higher fields than even the CH₃ absorption.

In some cases, a temperature effect on chemical shifts may result from changes in amplitude of torsional vibrations with temperature. An example is 1,1,2,2-tetrafluoro-3-phenylcyclobutane, which shows substantial changes in the chemical shifts of the fluorine atoms as the temperature is increased or decreased because of changes in the amplitudes of vibration of the fluorines with respect to each other and the aromatic ring at the 3-position.[3]

Studies of the proton resonance absorptions of a wide variety of organic compounds have revealed that the resonance lines for similarly located hydrogens appear at comparable applied magnetic fields. This fact permits setting up a table of δ values for various types of protons as is shown in Table 2–1. The line positions for a given species of

[2] A. D. Cohen and C. Reid, *J. Chem. Phys.,* **25,** 790 (1956).
[3] Unpublished experiments by W. D. Phillips and coworkers.

hydrogen are seen to occur over a moderate range of values as would depend on the electrical and shielding effects of substituent groups as well as bulk diamagnetic shielding influences produced by the other molecules in the sample. Recent work has shown that variations in δ because of the latter factor can be minimized by extrapolating the line positions to infinite dilution in a suitable common solvent [4a] or by using internal standards.[4b] For best results, internal standards should be chosen to be of such nature that any bulk diamagnetic shielding effects are expected to influence the resonances of the sample and standard to the same degree. The internal standard procedure is very convenient and has been shown by Chamberlain [4b] to narrow the range of variations in δ values for many of the individual types of proton resonances listed in Table 2–1 to less than $\pm 0.2 \times 10^6$.

Some idea of the magnitude of solvent effects on chemical shifts is provided by the data of Table 2–2 which show the change in δ for methyl protons in a variety of compounds between pure liquid and extrapolated to infinite dilution in carbon tetrachloride.[5] In general, the changes are large and irregular enough to suggest need for considerable caution in interpreting pure liquid spectra. Changes of chemical shift in some solvents appear to parallel changes in bulk diamagnetic susceptibility.[5]

A cursory examination of Table 2–1 might lead one to believe that there is a relationship between the δ value of a proton and its acidity. This is not an unreasonable idea, since the electron density is important in determining both the diamagnetic shielding and the ease of removal of the proton by bases. Thus, a sulfonic acid proton appears at very low fields as would be expected if the electron density and diamagnetic shielding of the acidic proton were small. Carboxyl protons come at higher fields while water and alcohol protons are near the center of the table. Furthermore, the very weakly acidic amine and hydrocarbon protons come at the end of the table, corresponding to high electron densities and high diamagnetic shielding. However, closer inspection of Table 2–1 shows a number of groups, the proton δ values of which cannot be fitted into any simple acidity scale. Thus, aldehydic hydrogens appear at quite low fields, as do aromatic hydrogens. In contrast, the relatively strongly acidic acetylenic hydrogens come at rather high fields.

[4a] A. A. Bothner-By and R. E. Glick, *J. Chem. Phys.*, **26**, 1651 (1957); [4b] N. F. Chamberlain, *Anal. Chem.* (in press).

[5] A. L. Allred and E. G. Rochow, *J. Am. Chem. Soc.*, **79**, 5363 (1957).

Table 2–2.   Change in δ for Methyl Protons between Pure Liquid and Infinite Dilution in Carbon Tetrachloride *

Compound	δ (pure liquid)	δ (infinite dilution in CCl₄)	Δ
CH_3NO_2	+1.19	+0.48	−0.71
CH_3F	2.10	0.53	−1.57
$CH_3OC_6H_5$	1.83	1.09	−0.74
CH_3OH	1.85	1.39	−0.46
CH_3OCH_3	2.63	1.55	−1.08
CH_3Cl	2.10	1.74	−0.36
CH_3Br	2.02	2.10	+0.08
CH_3I	2.00	2.60	+0.60
CH_3CN	3.14	2.89	−0.25
$(CH_3)_4C$	4.35	3.84	−0.51

* Data from Allred and Rochow.[5]

2-4.   Chemical Shifts for Other Nuclei

Generally speaking, the chemical shifts for most magnetic nuclei are much larger than for hydrogen. Representative δ values for ^{17}O and ^{14}N are given in Table 2–3; these have a greater spread than the proton δ values by a factor of about 100. The decisive factor with these nuclei

Table 2–3.   Typical ^{17}O and ^{14}N δ Values ($\times 10^6$) *

H_2O	0	$NH_4\oplus$	+602
RONO	−170	N_2H_4	+566
RCO_2H	−220	NH_3	+544
$HCONH_2$	−320	CH_3CONH_2	+498
RONO	−380	RCN	+385
SO_2	−540	C_5H_5N	+276
$(CH_3)_2CO$	−600	$C_6H_5NO_2$	+252
RNO_2	−640	$NO_2\ominus$	0

* Data from B. E. Holder and M. P. Klein, *J. Chem. Phys.*, **23**, 1956 (1955), and H. E. Weaver, B. M. Tolbert, and R. C. La Force, *J. Chem. Phys.*, **23**, 1956 (1955).

is probably the greater polarizability of the electrons in the L shell as compared to those in the K shell. Chemical shifts associated with ^{13}C have also been measured for a variety of simple organic compounds by Lauterbur and Holm,[6] using ^{13}C of natural abundance. A fairly special technique is necessary, and rather large samples are required. Nonetheless, the shifts are large, as with ^{14}N and ^{17}O, and many chemical applications of the ^{13}C resonances can be foreseen.

2-5. Proton δ Values and Electronegativity

Chemical shifts are of considerable value in structural investigations involving nuclei in different locations. Several examples of such uses of proton chemical shifts will be described shortly, but first we shall consider possible correlations between δ and other structural parameters, since much effort has been expended in this direction. Most important are attempted correlations of δ with electronegativities and some parameters which have been shown to be useful in defining chemical reactivities. From the earlier discussions regarding the relation between chemical shift and electron density, one would expect electronegativity effects to be displayed by substituent groups, so placed as to influence the electron density around a given nucleus. Of course, the substituent or substituents can act also to change the chemical shift by effectively making a change in the solvent as well.

Dailey and Shoolery [7] have studied substituent effects in ethyl derivatives by determining differences in chemical shifts between the methylene and methyl protons as a function of X for CH_3CH_2X. The system is a particularly desirable one because the effect of X in altering the medium would be expected to be nearly the same at the two positions. An excellent correlation was noticed between the difference in resonance line positions for CH_3 and CH_2 protons of ethyl halides and the Huggins electronegativity values. The relationship was nicely linear (see Fig. 2-3) although there seems to be no real a priori reason for expecting this to be the case. With the aid of the linear relationship and chemical shifts for the protons of other ethyl derivatives, apparent electronegativities were assigned to a wide variety of substituent groups. The ultimate worth of the figures so obtained is yet to be demonstrated through correlation with other properties related to electronegativities.

    [6] P. C. Lauterbur, *J. Chem. Phys.*, **26**, 217 (1957) and *Ann. N.Y. Acad. Sci.*, **70**, 841 (1958); C. H. Holm, *J. Chem. Phys.*, **26**, 707 (1957).

    [7] B. P. Dailey and J. N. Shoolery, *J. Am. Chem. Soc.*, **77**, 3977 (1955). Similar measurements have been made by Allred and Rochow.[5]

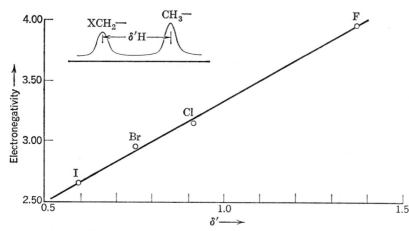

Fig. 2-3. Chemical shift between CH₂ and CH₃ protons of ethyl halides as a function of the Huggins electronegativity values. (*Courtesy of B. P. Dailey and the Journal of the American Chemical Society.*)

2-6.   δ and Hammett's σ Constants

Considerable work has been done over the last 30 years on chemical reactivities of aromatic compounds. Hammett [8] has shown how much of the resulting data for reactivities of groups connected to benzene rings carrying substituents in the meta and para positions can be correlated with the aid of parameters σ (substituent) and ϱ (reaction).

$$\log \frac{k_1}{k_0} = \sigma\varrho$$

Each substituent can usually be assigned a σ constant the value of which depends on whether the substituent is located at a meta or para position. In turn, each reaction may be assigned a ϱ parameter which measures the sensitivity of its rate to changes of substituents in the meta and para positions. The reaction parameter turns out to be a function of temperature, solvent, salt concentrations, and the character of the reagents employed. Hammett's relationship holds with very considerable precision for the ionization constants of meta- and para-substituted benzoic acids and the alkaline saponification rates of the corresponding ethyl esters. With its aid, one can compute many thousands of individual rates and equilibrium constants from rather small tables of substituent and reaction parameters. Hammett's σ constants are of particular interest to the present discussion and are taken normally to represent the

[8] L. P. Hammett, "Physical Organic Chemistry," chap. 7, McGraw-Hill Book Company, Inc., New York, 1940.

difference in the logarithms of the ionization constants of the meta- or para-substituted benzoic acids and benzoic acid itself.

Numerous attempts have been made to correlate σ with various physical properties, such as polarographic reduction potentials, infrared vibration frequencies, and wavelengths of maximum absorption in electronic spectra. Gutowsky and coworkers [9] have published data on the chemical shifts of a large number of meta- and para-substituted fluorobenzenes which are of considerable pertinence to the correlation of δ values with chemical reactivity parameters. Figure 2-4 shows the degree of correlation of fluorine δ values with Hammett's σ constants,

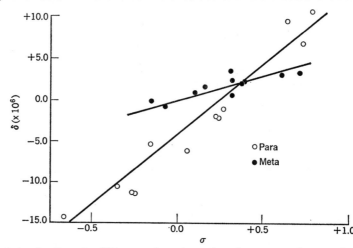

Fig. 2-4. δ values for ^{19}F resonance absorptions in meta- and para-substituted fluorobenzenes as a function of Hammett's substituent constant σ. (*After Gutowsky and coworkers.*)

and it is immediately clear that a different relationship holds from that customarily observed for chemical equilibrium and rate constants. In the first place, the points corresponding to substituents at meta positions fall along a line of substantially different slope from the best line drawn through the points for substituents located at para positions. This behavior has no exact parallel in chemical-reactivity studies.

Gutowsky interprets the data of Fig. 2-4 to mean that the resonance effects of substituent groups are more important in determining chemical shifts than are the other factors that make up the over-all electrical effect. The observed scatter of the points is expected on this basis, since the resonance contribution is already included for each substituent in

[9] H. S. Gutowsky, D. W. McCall, B. R. McGarvey, and L. H. Meyer, *J. Am. Chem. Soc.,* **74,** 4809 (1952).

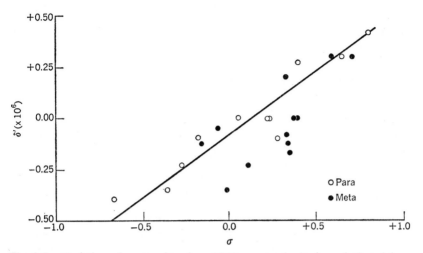

Fig. 2-5. Variation of proton δ' values (C_6H_{12} as standard) for substituted benzenes with Hammett's σ constants.

the σ constants, at least to the extent that it influences chemical reactivity. Taft [10] has evaluated the resonance contributions of substituents to their σ constants and has corroborated Gutowsky's suggestion that resonance effects are particularly important in determining the influence of substituents on fluorine δ values.

The situation for protons is not quite so simple. Dailey [11] and Bothner-By [4] and coworkers have measured proton chemical shifts for a variety of benzenoid compounds. Some typical data are presented in Fig. 2-5, and it is seen that there is no simple relationship between σ and δ. Furthermore, no obvious tendency exists for the meta and para points to lie along lines with different slopes as is observed with substituted fluorobenzenes.

It is possible that some of the above anomalies may be due to abnormal diamagnetic shielding effects produced by the unsaturation electrons of the benzene ring, since when an aromatic compound is placed in a magnetic field, the π electrons circulate around the ring so as to produce a rather substantial local magnetic field directed normal to the ring which can influence the chemical shift. Waugh [12] has shown with 1,4-decamethylenebenzene that the position of each methylene group with respect to the circulating current of electrons above and below the ring is quite critical in determining the chemical shift of the methylene

[10] R. W. Taft, Jr., *J. Am. Chem. Soc., 79,* 1045 (1957).
[11] P. L. Corio and B. P. Dailey, *J. Am. Chem. Soc., 78,* 3043 (1957).
[12] J. S. Waugh and R. W. Fessenden, *J. Am. Chem. Soc., 79,* 846 (1957).

protons. The apparently abnormal chemical shift of acetylenic protons may be due to circulation of the unsaturation electrons around the axis of the triple bond in such a way as to set up a local field which opposes the applied field along the triple bond, thus causing more shielding than is normal for an unsaturated atom.

2-7.   Resonance Signal Areas and Widths

For use of NMR spectra as an aid to quantitative analysis and structure determinations, it is important to consider the limitations of the relationship between the magnitude of the nuclear resonance signal and the number of nuclei involved. In the first place, for a given kind of nuclei, the area under the resonance curve is expected to be closely proportional to the number of nuclei involved in the absence of large solvent effects. Thus, one should be able to determine the amount of benzene in mixtures with cyclohexane by measuring the area under the benzene peak and employing a single calibration mixture, provided that the volume of the material in the receiver coil was the same in each case. Another way of making such an analysis would be to take the ratio between the areas under the benzene and cyclohexane peaks. With very sharp peaks, a rough analysis may also be possible on the basis of peak heights, but this is not to be regarded as a generally satisfactory procedure unless the resonance lines have exactly the same width.

In general, the width of a resonance line is usually determined by the relaxation time T_2 so that the width at one-half of the full signal strength is numerically equal to $1/T_2$ (cf. discussion on page 97). Here, we distinguish between the intrinsic relaxation time of the sample and the relaxation time which results from use of a nonhomogeneous external magnetic field. The line width which can be ascribed to the sample itself is sometimes called the "natural line width," and for many non-viscous substances it is smaller than can be achieved even with the most homogeneous magnetic fields now available. Line widths can often be reduced by spinning the sample in the magnetic field with the aid of an air turbine or some similar device. This has the effect of averaging out the field inhomogeneities perpendicular to the direction of spinning and, as is seen in Fig. 2-6, produces a very notable sharpening of the spectrum. An apparatus which permits thermostating of a spinning sample is shown in Fig. 2-7.

Under conditions of "slow passage" through a nuclear resonance spectrum (see Appendix A), the areas under the peaks are approximately proportional to the number of nuclei and $(1 + H_1^2 T_1 T_2 \gamma^2)^{-\frac{1}{2}}$ where H_1 is the magnitude of the rotating field vector. Consequently,

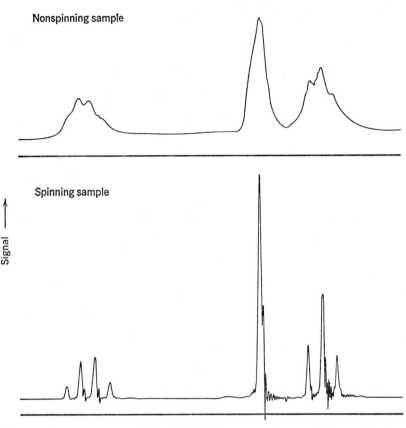

Nonspinning sample

Spinning sample

Signal ———>

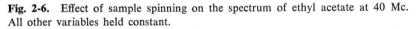

Magnetic field sweep ———>

Fig. 2-6.   Effect of sample spinning on the spectrum of ethyl acetate at 40 Mc. All other variables held constant.

when the oscillator field strength is large and the relaxation times long, so that $H_1^2 T_1 T_2 \gamma^2 \geq 1$, the areas will be a function of the relaxation times and H_1. This will be important not only for nuclei with different relaxation times because of different chemical locations (as for protons on the ring or side-chain of toluene), but also for those located in equivalent molecular positions and subjected to different solvent influences as might change the relaxation times.

The importance of relaxation times on resonance signal areas under slow-passage conditions can be reduced by operating at low oscillator field strengths or, better, by extrapolating the ratio of the areas at several oscillator strengths to zero. However, this does not necessarily solve the signal-area problem, since slow passage is not generally practical

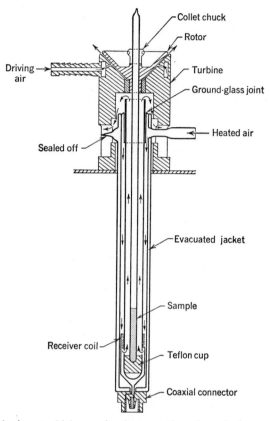

Fig. 2-7.   Probe insert which permits thermostating of a spinning sample. (*Courtesy of Review of Scientific Instruments.*)

for the determination of high-resolution spectra of organic liquids. In analysis of multicomponent systems, appropriate corrections can be made empirically with suitable calibration graphs. A much more serious problem may arise in structure determinations when one requires ratios of numbers of nuclei in different chemical locations for a given substance. For example, *t*-butylbenzene as an unknown could be distinguished from tetramethylbenzene by showing that the ratio between aliphatic and aromatic hydrogens is 9:5 for one and 12:2 for the other. Such a structure proof is unambiguous, provided the differences in relaxation times between the aromatic and aliphatic hydrogens are not so great as to cause the resonance signal areas to differ greatly from the theoretical values. An example of the kind of difficulties sometimes encountered is provided by cyclobutene, which gives areas under the methylene and double-bond hydrogen resonances as high as 2.8:1 (vs. the theoretical 2:1) even at low oscillator strengths.

2-8. Chemical Shifts and Organic Structure Determinations. General Considerations

a. Feist's Acid

Measurements of chemical shifts and signal areas can be extremely valuable in determinations of structures of both simple and complicated molecules. An example is Feist's acid, originally postulated by Thorpe and coworkers,[13] to be a methylcyclopropenedicarboxylic acid on the basis of chemical evidence—particularly, ozonization of the diethyl ester, which gave no formaldehyde but only a substance having properties appropriate to diethyl oxaloacetoacetate. Later, Ettlinger [14] showed that a more likely structure for Feist's acid was *trans*-3-methylenecyclopropane-1,2-dicarboxylic acid.

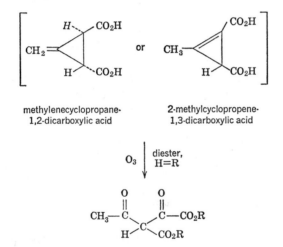

methylenecyclopropane-
1,2-dicarboxylic acid   2-methylcyclopropene-
1,3-dicarboxylic acid

Feist's acid is a high-melting solid, and satisfactory high-resolution spectra are usually obtainable only with nonviscous liquids or solutions. This is because in solid or viscous materials, the intermolecular magnetic effects of the various magnetic nuclei on one another are substantial and produce local variations in the total magnetic field. These result in a spread of precession frequencies even for nuclei of the same chemical kind, and such a spread in precession frequencies causes line-

[13] F. R. Goss, C. K. Ingold, and J. F. Thorpe, *J. Chem. Soc.*, **123**, 327 (1923).
[14] M. G. Ettlinger, *J. Am. Chem. Soc.*, **74**, 5805 (1952).

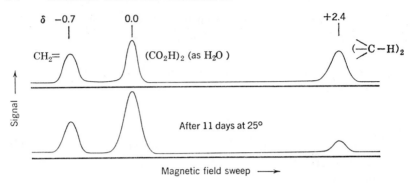

Fig. 2-8. Proton NMR spectrum of Feist's acid in deuterium oxide containing excess sodium deuteroxide.

broadening. In a nonviscous liquid, the molecules tumble over and over at a rapid rate and the effect of magnetic nuclei in one molecule on the precession frequencies of nuclei in another molecule is averaged to zero.

The choice of a suitable solvent for determination of the NMR spectra of Feist's acid or similar substances illustrates several points of practical importance. Ideally, the solvent would have no resonance absorption of its own or else only a single line such as might serve as a calibration point. Carbon tetrachloride and carbon disulfide are common nonhydrogenous organic solvents in which, unfortunately, most polar organic compounds have only a limited solubility. A number of substances are available with only a single proton absorption, such as chloroform, acetone, benzene, cyclohexane, dimethyl sulfoxide, dioxane, and water, which nicely cover the range between polar and nonpolar solvents. However, even with these solvents, if the sample is only partly soluble, the increase in receiver sensitivity necessary to obtain a measurable signal may well produce a troublesome, large, and broad solvent peak. This can be avoided by using suitably deuterated solvents, and many of these, such as deuterochloroform, benzene, acetic acid, acetone, and, of course, heavy water, are commercially available. In general, concentrated solutions are desirable to give a good signal-to-noise ratio and to diminish the importance of signals due to solvent impurities.

The proton resonance spectrum of Feist's acid was found to be most conveniently measured with the substance in the form of the sodium salt as obtained by dissolution in sodium deuteroxide–deuterium oxide solution.[15] Use of D_2O avoided a strong water peak and, in addition, gave a convenient calibration peak for the spectrum, because a two-proton water (or HDO) peak results from neutralization of the two

[15] A. T. Bottini and J. D. Roberts, *J. Org. Chem.*, **21**, 1169 (1956).

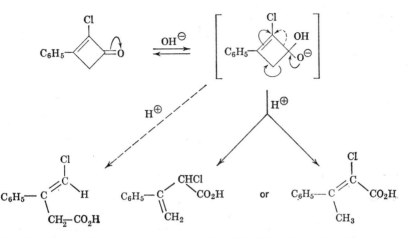

Fig. 2-9. Reasonable routes for ring opening of 2-chloro-3-phenylcyclobutenone.

carboxyl groups of the acid. As will be seen from Fig. 2-8, two other hydrogen resonances are observed. One of these appears in the vinyl hydrogen region as evinced by its δ value of -0.7×10^6, while the other comes at a much higher field strength ($\delta = +2.4 \times 10^6$). The areas of all three peaks are approximately the same, indicating that each corresponds to two protons. The NMR spectrum of Feist's acid is decisive with respect to a choice between the Thorpe and Ettlinger structures. The Ettlinger structure is in complete agreement with the observed spectrum, while the Thorpe structure would require aliphatic methyl and alicyclic ring hydrogen resonances at high fields in the ratio of 3:1 and no vinyl hydrogen resonance.

The study of Feist's acid gave a bonus observation in that the water peaks of the sodium deuteroxide solution (which contained some excess sodium deuteroxide) increased on standing at room temperature while the alicyclic hydrogen peaks decreased (see Fig. 2-8). This shows that the aliphatic hydrogens but not vinyl hydrogens exchanged slowly with the sodium deuteroxide–deuterium oxide solution at room temperature and, furthermore, proves that Feist's acid is not in rapid equilibrium under these conditions with molecules having the methylcyclopropenedicarboxylic acid structure because, in that case, the vinyl hydrogens would exchange as well.

Ettlinger [16] has used the same technique to show that exchange of the vinyl hydrogens does occur at higher temperatures, and this is the first evidence that molecules with the Thorpe structure can be formed at all.

[16] M. G. Ettlinger and F. Kennedy, *Chem. & Ind.* (*London*), 891 (1957).

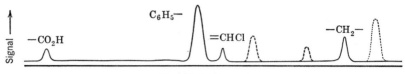

Fig. 2-10. Proton resonance spectrum of 4-chloro-3-phenyl-3-butenoic acid from the base-induced ring opening of 2-chloro-3-phenylcyclobutenone. Dashed line (-----) shows high-field peaks expected for 2-chloro-3-phenyl-3-butenoic acid. Dotted line (· · · ·) shows expected position of methyl resonance for 2-chloro-3-phenyl-2-butenoic acid.

b. Ring-opening Reaction of 2-Chloro-3-phenylcyclobutenone

Another structure proof utilizing the same principles involves the phenylchlorobutenoic acid formed from ring opening of 2-chloro-3-phenylcyclobutenone with sodium hydroxide.[17] Reasonable mechanisms leading to three isomeric acids can be written for this reaction, and a priori one might expect that formation of the conjugated isomer 2-chloro-3-phenylbutenoic acid would be favored (see Fig. 2-9). The NMR spectrum (Fig. 2-10) of the reaction product indicates otherwise. Besides the carboxyl and phenyl hydrogen resonances which would be common to all three of the reasonably expected structures, there are two other peaks in the ratio of 1:2. The one-hydrogen resonance occurs in the vinyl hydrogen region, while the two-hydrogen resonance is at somewhat lower fields than a normal aliphatic hydrogen. We thus conclude that the product is 4-chloro-3-phenyl-3-butenoic acid formed by breaking the cyclobutenone ring between the 1- and 2-positions. The a priori expected structure is ruled out, since it would show no vinyl hydrogens and a simple three-hydrogen methyl resonance in the aliphatic hydrogen region. The line positions alone do not serve to rule out 2-chloro-3-phenyl-3-butenoic acid as a possibility, since it has both the vinyl- and aliphatic-type hydrogens, but the ratios of high-to-low field resonance lines for this compound would be reversed from what is actually observed.

c. Complex Organic Structures

The use of nuclear magnetic resonance can be profitably extended to even quite complex naturally occurring substances. An example taken from steroid chemistry is the tetracyclic ketol obtained by Johnson and coworkers [18] by way of an aldol condensation and assigned the structure shown below by virtue of its conversion through the action of strong

[17] E. F. Silversmith, Y. Kitahara, M. C. Caserio, and J. D. Roberts, *J. Am. Chem. Soc.*, in press.

[18] W. S. Johnson and coworkers, *J. Am. Chem. Soc.*, **78**, 6302 (1956).

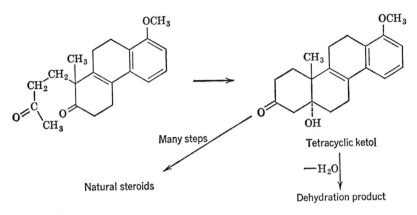

Natural steroids

Many steps

Tetracyclic ketol

$-H_2O$

Dehydration product

base and then by a long sequence of synthetic steps to naturally occurring steroidal hormones.

A dehydration product derived from the ketol was found to have chemical and physical properties hard to reconcile with the given structure of the starting material. The NMR spectra of the ketol (as the acetate) and its dehydration product are shown in Fig. 2-11 with most of the principal resonance lines identified as belonging to the various structural entities. There are two prominent lines in the spectrum of the ketol which are of the appropriate height and position to correspond to $-\overset{|}{\underset{|}{C}}-CH_3$ groups. However, only one such absorption is expected on the basis of the postulated structure for the ketol. It is interesting that one of the $-\overset{|}{\underset{|}{C}}-CH_3$ groups disappears on dehydration.

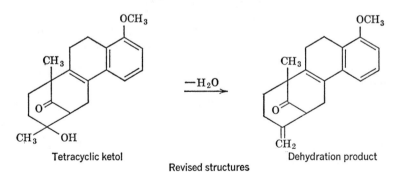

Tetracyclic ketol

$-H_2O$

Dehydration product

Revised structures

Reevaluation of the structure of the ketol on the basis of its NMR spectra has indicated that it and its dehydration product are best formulated as shown above.[19] Synthesis of natural steroidal hormones

[19] Private communication from W. S. Johnson.

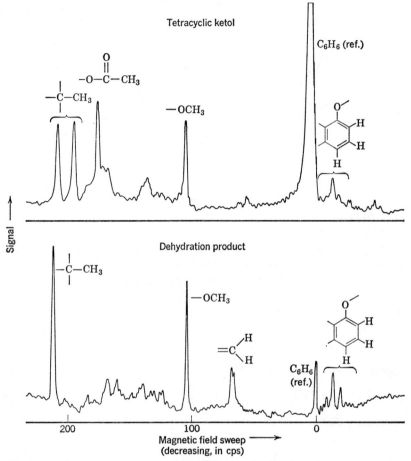

Fig. 2-11. Proton resonance spectra of tetracyclic ketol as its acetate and a corresponding dehydration product at 40 Mc. (*Courtesy of William S. Johnson.*)

from the ketol is possible because ring opening, recyclization, and dehydration occur under the influence of strong base.

Nuclear magnetic resonance spectra of a large number of steroidal

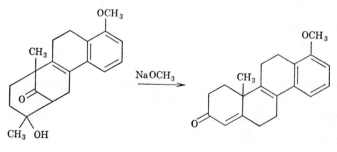

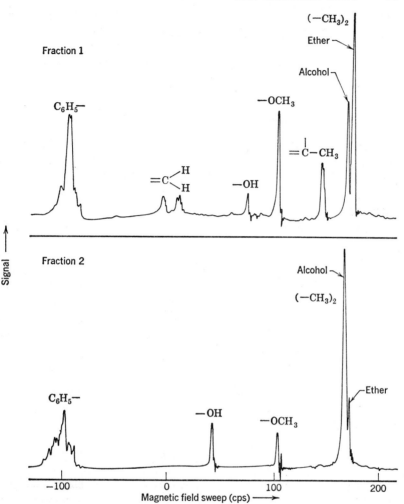

Fig. 2-12. Proton NMR spectra at 40 Mc of two fractions from an exploratory methylation of phenyldimethylcarbinol.

compounds have been analyzed by Shoolery and Rogers.[20] Interesting differences of about 20 cps were noted between axial and equatorial protons at the 3- and 11-positions of the steroid carbon skeleton.

A further elegant example of the use of NMR data for elucidation of complex organic structures is provided by the work of van Tamelen [21] on photosantonic acid. Here, a key finding was of a vinyl-proton resonance

[20] J. N. Shoolery and M. T. Rogers, *J. Am. Chem. Soc.*, **80**, 5121 (1958).
[21] E. E. van Tamelen, S. H. Levin, G. Brenner, J. Wolinsky, and P. Aldrich, *J. Am. Chem. Soc.*, **80**, 501 (1958).

which could not be accommodated by most of the proposed structures. The spectrum will be discussed further in Chap. 3 in connection with spin-spin splitting, since, besides its characteristic chemical shift, the vinyl proton resonance showed other features which give strong support to van Tamelen's structure for photosantonic acid.

2-9.   Illustrative Analysis of a Reaction Product

Nuclear magnetic resonance spectra are often useful for characterization of complex reaction mixtures. For example, in an exploratory methylation of phenyldimethylcarbinol, distillation of the reaction products gave two principal fractions with NMR spectra as shown in Fig. 2-12. These spectra can be quite well analyzed even without the aid of separate spectra of the pure components.[22] The presence of resonance lines in the vinyl hydrogen region indicates the formation of some α-methylstyrene, while the band at $+100$ cps shows the presence of O–CH$_3$. The methyl absorptions of the ether are separated somewhat from those of the alcohol, and we can assign the higher of the two peaks in the first fraction to the ether, since it is roughly twice the O–CH$_3$ resonance. Each fraction shows O–H lines which are shifted somewhat from one fracton to the other by chemical shift changes associated with solvent changes as explained earlier for ethanol. From the NMR spectra, we can conclude that the first and second fractions have approximately the compositions 53 and 23 per cent methyl phenyldimethylcarbinyl ether, 35 and 77 per cent phenyldimethylcarbinol, and 12 and 0 per cent α-methylstyrene, respectively.

2-10.   Accentuation of Chemical Shifts by Paramagnetic Salts

Phillips and coworkers [23] have shown how in favorable cases chemical shifts can be greatly and selectively accentuated by paramagnetic salts. For example, 1.0 M cobaltous chloride dissolved in n-propyl alcohol causes the various proton resonances to separate rather widely from one another. The O–H line remains about in its usual position, but the α-methylene proton resonance is shifted some 200 cps to higher fields at 7,050 gauss. The shift is proportional to the applied magnetic field and, for a long-chain alcohol such as 1-hexanol, increases as one goes down the chain to higher numbered carbons until a maximum is

---

[22] Unpublished experiments by M. C. Caserio.
[23] W. D. Phillips, C. E. Looney, and C. K. Ikeda, *J. Chem. Phys.*, **27**, 1435 (1957).

reached at and beyond the 3-position. The differences in chemical shift for the various kinds of hydrogens depend on the paramagnetic cobaltous ion being coordinated by the alcohol molecules at the hydroxyl oxygen. It seems likely that studies of this character may give valuable information as to the conformation of organic molecules in solution.

CHAPTER 3

Spin-Spin Splitting

3-1. The High-resolution Ethanol Spectrum

The spectrum of ethanol shown in Fig. 2-1 was obtained with a degree of resolution far below that routinely possible for commercial NMR spectrometers. Under high resolution, the proton spectra of ethyl derivatives show a considerably greater number of lines—the CH_2 resonance being split into four principal lines and the CH_3 resonance into three principal lines. Still higher resolution such as is possible with an extremely stable oscillator and a highly homogeneous magnetic field shows each of these lines to have fine structure, as shown in Fig. 3-1. We shall be concerned here only with the first-order splitting, since the explanation of the higher-order splitting is rather involved.

The mechanism by which the protons of an ethyl group produce five major resonance lines is interesting and important to theories of structure as well as structural determinations. In the first place, one might infer that the splitting of the CH_2 and CH_3 lines is evidence for *chem-*

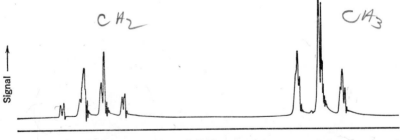

Fig. 3-1. High-resolution spectrum of ethyl group protons of acidified ethanol at 40 Mc. (*Courtesy of James N. Shoolery and Varian Associates.*)

42

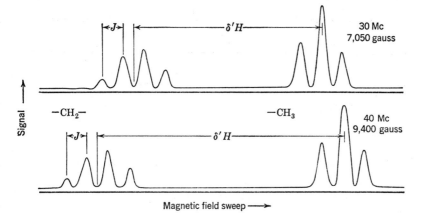

Fig. 3-2. Change of NMR spectrum of typical ethyl group protons under moderate resolution as a function of field strength.

ically different kinds of methylene and methyl hydrogens. However, the fine structure is not a chemical-shift phenomenon. This is proved by observing the spectrum at two different oscillator frequencies (and field strengths) whereby the principal lines of the methyl and methylene patterns move closer together or farther apart while the spacing of the principal four-three pattern of fine structure remains unaltered, as shown in Fig. 3-2. Therefore, we conclude that the different lines are not due to chemically different hydrogens among the methylene and methyl groups, respectively. This conclusion is, of course, in agreement with chemical experience. It can be shown that field-independent splitting represented by the line spacing J arises from interaction between the magnetic moments of one group of hydrogens and the other. The way that this comes about will be illustrated with the aid of a simple but experimentally unrealizable example.

3-2.   Spin-Spin Splitting in a Single Crystal

Consider a single crystal made up of H–D molecules, all of which are so oriented that the lines connecting the nuclei of the individual molecules make an angle θ with an applied magnetic field (Fig. 3-3). Now consider nuclear resonance absorption by deuterium nuclei located at position 1. Each deuteron precesses in a field whose magnitude is determined partly by the applied field and partly by the degree of diamagnetic shielding produced by the bonding electrons. However, this is not the whole story, since each deuterium nucleus will be connected to a proton (at position 2) which can have either of the two

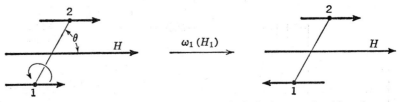

Fig. 3-3. A molecule of H–D in a hypothetical single crystal subjected to an applied magnetic field H and a suitable oscillator frequency ω_1 to cause nucleus 1 to absorb rf energy.

possible magnetic quantum numbers, $+\frac{1}{2}$ or $-\frac{1}{2}$. If the proton nuclear magnet is oriented in the direction of the magnetic field, then it will augment the field which is experienced by the adjacent deuteron and the total field at the deuteron will correspond to a higher precession frequency than if the proton had no nuclear moment. If the proton magnet is directed the other way, the field at the deuterium nucleus will be reduced from its nominal value. Therefore, the precession frequency of a given deuterium and the position of its resonance lines will depend on the magnetic quantum number of the proton to which it is bonded. In a large assemblage of H–D molecules, there will be almost precisely equal numbers of protons with the two possible spin quantum numbers, even in an intense applied field, unless the temperature is so low that thermal agitation cannot prevent an appreciable excess of the nuclei from being lined up with the applied field. Consequently, at ordinary temperatures, very nearly half of the H–D molecules will show a deuteron resonance at a lower field strength than would be the case if the proton moment were absent, while the other half of the molecules will have their deuterium resonance at a correspondingly higher field strength. The observed spectrum will then appear somewhat as in Fig. 3-4.

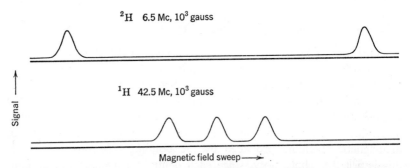

Fig. 3-4. Expected NMR spectrum for a single crystal of H–D molecules assuming negligible intermolecular magnetic interactions.

The proton resonance spectrum will be affected by the deuterons in an analogous way, except that, since the deuteron has $I = 1$ and three possible magnetic quantum numbers $(+1, 0, -1)$, the proton resonances will occur at three field strengths. Since the probability that a given deuteron will have any one of the magnetic quantum numbers is essentially one-third, the three lines will be of equal height. It can be shown theoretically that the interaction between the spins is such that the spacing of the deuteron and proton resonance lines depends on the ratios of the gyromagnetic ratios of the nuclei. A rough calculation for an H–D crystal with $\theta = 90°$ shows the predicted spacing of the deuteron resonances to be about 35 gauss, so that proton resonances would be separated by $35 \times \gamma_D/\gamma_H$, or 5.3 gauss. This type of magnetic interaction between nuclei is usually called "spin-spin splitting." Since magnetic coupling between nuclei causes changes in precession frequencies depending on the magnitude of the nuclear moment but not the external field, it is clear that the magnitude of the splitting should be independent of the applied field.

Magnetic interaction among nuclei as postulated for the hypothetical crystal of H–D molecules is "direct dipole-dipole interaction" and leads to a line separation proportional to $(3 \cos^2 \theta - 1)r^{-3}$ with θ as defined earlier and r the distance between the nuclei. In crystals, besides the intramolecular nuclear interactions, one will expect also substantial intermolecular dipole-dipole interactions leading to additional splittings or broadening of the absorption lines (see earlier discussion, page 33).

3-3.   Spin-Spin Splitting in Liquids

If our hypothetical single crystal of H–D molecules were allowed to melt, the restraints between the molecules would diminish and rapid molecular tumbling would begin. Tumbling molecules present all possible values of the angle θ between the internuclear lines and the magnetic field axis. Integration of $(3 \cos^2 \theta - 1)$ over all possible values of θ shows that the time-average direct dipole-dipole interaction between the bonded H–D nuclei is zero. Hence, we would expect that there would then be no observable spin-spin coupling in nuclear resonance spectra of liquids or gases. Nonetheless, small couplings persist even when tumbling is rapid, although they are usually on the order of about 10^{-2} gauss, roughly $\frac{1}{1,000}$ of the values expected for direct dipole-dipole interactions. The residual couplings are not merely due to partial averaging of the dipole-dipole interaction through tumbling, since they are temperature independent except in special cases. It has been shown that the residual couplings are the result of magnetic interactions transmitted between nuclei by the bonding electrons in such a way as not to be averaged to zero by tumbling.

Except that the lines are much narrower and very much more closely spaced, the appearance of the NMR spectrum given by tumbling H–D molecules is qualitatively the same as predicted for the single crystal, i.e., a doublet deuteron resonance and a triplet proton resonance. The argument for expecting this pattern is unchanged from that given earlier for the crystal except that now the influence of the magnetic orientation of one nucleus on the precession frequency of the other nucleus is considered to be transmitted by the bonding electrons instead of by direct dipole-dipole interaction.

Gutowsky, McCall, and Slichter [1] discuss the relation between the magnitudes of spin-spin interactions among nuclei as a function of various atomic and molecular parameters. Customarily, spin-spin coupling constants are found to decrease monotonically with the number of chemical bonds between the nuclei involved. Several spectacular failures of this generalization have been observed involving fluorine-fluorine and hydrogen-fluorine interactions. For example, it has been found that the coupling between hydrogen and fluorine atoms connected to the 1 and 3 carbons of certain cyclobutene derivatives, and thus four chemical bonds apart, are much larger than the corresponding interactions between the same groups attached to the 1 and 4 carbons, which are only three bonds apart.[2] Similarly, the hydrogens on the 1 and 3

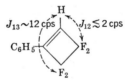

carbons of bromoallene (four bonds apart) are coupled more strongly even than the CH_2 and CH_3 hydrogens of an ethyl group (three bonds apart).

3-4. Spin-Spin Splitting in the Ethyl Group

The typical three-four line resonance pattern of the ethyl group arises because of spin-spin coupling between the methyl and methylene protons. It turns out that the coupling constant J, which represents the line spacings, is very nearly constant over a wide range of ethyl derivatives and amounts to about 1.6 milligauss or 7 cps.

[1] H. S. Gutowsky, D. W. McCall, and C. P. Slichter, *J. Chem. Phys.*, **21**, 279 (1953).

[2] C. M. Sharts and J. D. Roberts, *J. Am. Chem. Soc.*, **79**, 1008 (1957).

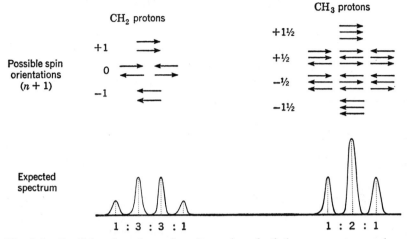

Fig. 3-5. Possible orientations of nuclear spins of ethyl group protons and expected spin-spin splitting pattern.

Reference to Fig. 3-5 shows that the two methylene protons may have any one of four possible combinations of their magnetic quantum numbers. Thus, both magnetic quantum numbers may be the same with either a $+$ or $-$ sign for the total or they may be different (two possible ways) and cancel each other's magnetic effect. The ethyl groups from molecule to molecule can then be classified into those in which the total spin of the methylene protons adds to $+1$, those in which they cancel each other, and those in which they add to -1. The methyl protons in ethyl groups whose methylene protons have a total spin of $+1$ will come into resonance when the magnetic field is increasing sooner than the others. When the methylene protons have a net spin of zero, they will have no effect on the resonance line position of the methyl, while if the net spin is -1, the line will come late by the same amount as the $+1$ combination came early. Consequently, there should be a total of three resonance lines for the methyl group because of the adjacent methylene protons. Since there are a total of four equally probable combinations of the methylene magnetic quantum numbers, one way to give $+1$, two ways to give zero, and one way to give -1, it will be expected that the three resonance lines will have signal-strength ratios of 1:2:1. Similar reasoning applied to the resonance absorption of the methylene protons in the presence of the methyl protons leads to prediction of a four-line spectrum with the signal strengths in the ratio 1:3:3:1.

In the above analysis, the spins of a group of equivalent protons were taken to be independent (each with two possible orientations in the external field) and distributed statistically among the possible states as shown in Fig. 3-5. This procedure gives satisfactory predictions for many simple spin-spin splitting problems but fails in others. Chemically equivalent protons in a group like a methyl are actually coupled to one another to give, in effect, a larger magnet which in turn is coupled to the external field. Consequently, such protons are not to be expected to behave independently of one another in all situations. This point will be discussed further in Sec. 3-7.

3-5.   More Complex Spin-Spin Splittings

a. Styrene Oxide

In general, we shall anticipate that the resonance of a given nucleus will be split into $(n + 1)$ lines by n equivalently placed magnetic nuclei with $I = 1/2$. The situation is more complex if more than one J value is involved. Styrene oxide offers a nice example of three nonequivalent protons each coupled to the others with different J's. The spectrum of styrene oxide is shown in Fig. 3-6; the ring protons are not coupled to the side-chain protons, so only the latter will be considered. None of the side-chain protons are in equivalent chemical locations since one (α) is adjacent to the phenyl ring and the other two are either cis(β) or trans(β') to the phenyl ring. In the absence of spin-spin coupling, we would then expect a simple three-line proton spectrum as shown at the top of Fig. 3-6. The α proton will be coupled unequally to the β protons, and if we assume $J_{\alpha\beta}$ (trans) to be larger than $J_{\alpha\beta'}$ (cis), then four lines of roughly equal height will be observed for the α proton. The β protons are coupled to each other and in the first-order treatment would be expected to split each other's resonance so as to have four lines of equal strength. As will be shown later, the fact that the chemical-shift difference between the β protons $(\delta_{\beta\beta'}H)$ is not a great deal larger than the coupling constant $(J_{\beta\beta'})$ means that the lines are not all of equal height and the spacings between the centers of the groups are not $\delta_{\beta\beta'}H$ but $\sqrt{J_{\beta\beta'}{}^2 + (\delta_{\beta\beta'}H)^2}$. This, however, is a second-order effect which does not change the basic argument. Each line for the β protons will then be split by the coupling between the α and β protons with different J values, so that the β protons will give eight lines in all, as is clearly evident from the observed spectrum.

b. Aliphatic Alcohols

Nuclear spin-spin coupling and chemical-shift data are extremely useful for structural investigations. As an example, we may consider high-resolution NMR spectra of a number of simple aliphatic alcohols (Fig. 3-7). The signal strengths, line positions, and degrees of spin-spin

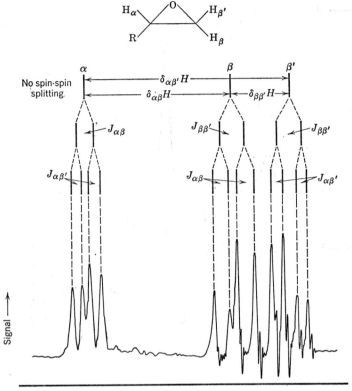

Fig. 3-6. Proton NMR spectra of styrene oxide at 40 Mc illustrating interaction between three nonequivalent protons. The resonance of the phenyl protons is off scale on the left.

splitting permit each alcohol to be identified unambiguously. Thus, isopropyl alcohol shows an O–H proton resonance, an α-proton resonance split into seven, and the resonance of six β protons split into a doublet. In the examples shown, the α hydrogens do not appear to be coupled to the hydroxyl protons, although there are only three bonds (H–C–O–H) separating them. The lack of this expected spin-spin splitting is a consequence of rapid intermolecular chemical exchange of the hydroxyl protons, as will be described later.

c. Methyl Photosantonate

The nuclear resonance spectrum of methyl photosantonate has been shown by van Tamelen [3] to be decisive in distinguishing among three

[3] E. E. van Tamelen, S. H. Levin, G. Brenner, J. Wolinsky, and P. Aldrich, *J. Am. Chem. Soc.*, **80**, 501 (1958), and private communication.

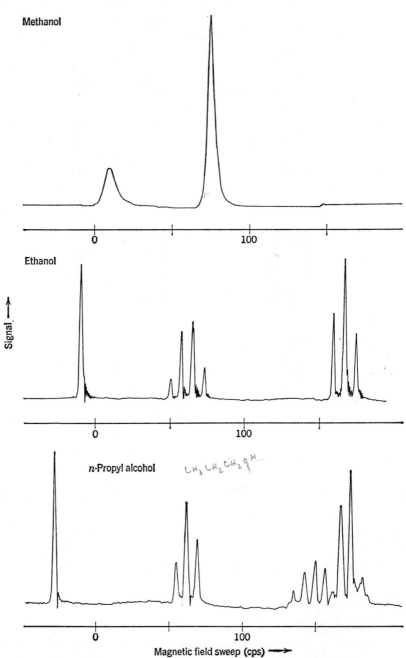

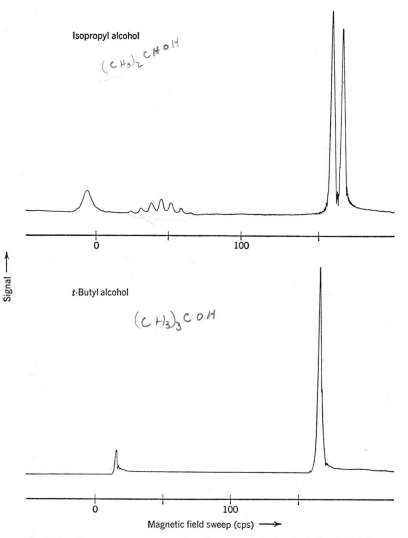

Fig. 3-7. Proton resonance spectra of some aliphatic alcohols at 40 Mc.

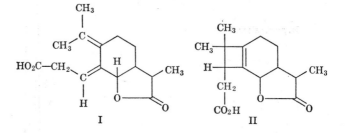

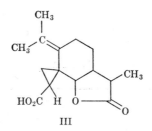

rather closely related proposed structures for photosantonic acid. An extraordinarily clear spectrum of the methyl ester at 60 Mc is shown in Fig. 3-8. The group of lines centered on 55 cps is in the vinyl hydrogen region and provides a telling argument in favor of structure I over struc-

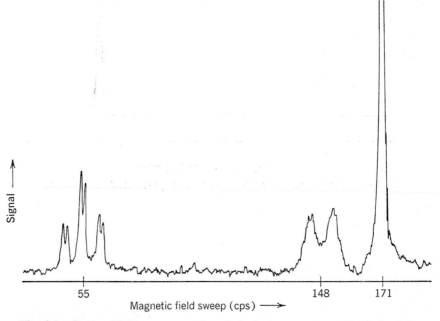

Fig. 3-8. Proton NMR spectrum of methyl photosantonate at 60 Mc in CCl₄.

tures II and III which have no vinyl hydrogens. Furthermore, the vinyl hydrogen resonance is split into three principal lines as would suggest the grouping $-CH_2-CH{=}C{<}$. This assignment is corroborated by the two principal lines centered on 216 cps which are in about the right place for a methylene group attached on one side to a carbomethoxy and on the other to a double bond. The spacing of these lines is identical with that observed for the vinyl hydrogen.

The slight doubling of the anticipated principal three-two pattern of the vinyl and methylene protons is invariant with the applied magnetic field and hence is the result of spin-spin coupling. Apparently, the side-chain $-CH_2-$ and $-CH{=}$ protons are coupled to the $>CH-O-$ proton with just sufficiently different J values to lead to only barely perceptible fine structure for the components of the 148-cps doublet.

3-6. Magnitudes of Coupling Constants

In saturated noncyclic compounds, spin-spin coupling constants for protons located on adjacent carbons (three bonds apart) are more or less constant from molecule to molecule at about 7 cps. Generally, J becomes immeasurably small with four bonds intervening, except when

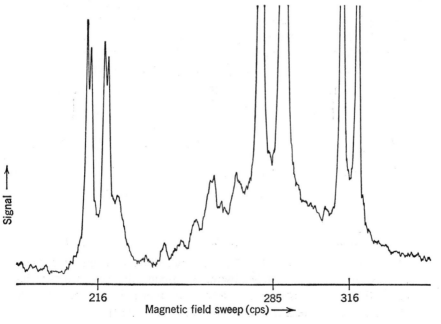

(*Courtesy of E. E. van Tamelen.*)

one or two of these is a double bond. Thus, as mentioned earlier, rather large couplings ($\sim$10 cps) are observed across the double bonds of an allenic system, and we note now that J is much smaller (1 to 2 cps) across one single and one double C–C bond, as in isobutylene.

An interesting variation of J with bond type has been noted by Shoolery[4] for couplings through the double bonds of a quinone and a derivative of the corresponding hydroquinone with a fully aromatic ring. Thus, the benzenoid thymol system shows no resolvable coupling between the ring protons and those on the adjacent alkyl groups whereas, with thymoquinone, one of the ring-proton resonances is split into a 1:3:3:1 quartet through spin-spin coupling involving the neighboring CH_3 group, while the other ring-proton resonance is split into a doublet by the α proton of the isopropyl group.

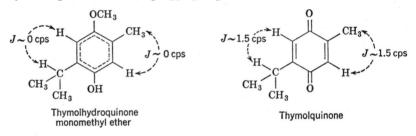

Thymolhydroquinone
monomethyl ether

Thymolquinone

Proton spin-spin couplings are powerfully influenced by molecular geometry. *Trans* conformations of protons in saturated compounds appear to lead to substantially larger couplings than corresponding *gauche* or eclipsed arrangements. Couplings between *trans* protons attached to double bonds are similarly larger than between *cis* protons.

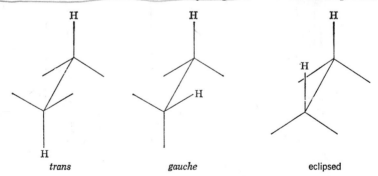

trans   *gauche*   eclipsed

In some compounds such as cyclobutene, spin-spin splitting is unexpectedly small or completely absent. Consequently, any structure interpretation which suggests that groups of nonequivalent protons are

[4] J. N. Shoolery, *Varian Associates Tech. Bull.,* **2,** 8 (1957).

not contiguous because of failure to observe spin-spin couplings may be seriously in error.

3-7.   Coupling between Equivalent and Nearly Equivalent Protons

In connection with spin-spin coupling in substances containing ethyl or similar groups, it is natural to wonder why there is no apparent splitting of the resonance of a proton belonging to an equivalent group of protons by the other members of the group, which are much closer than a group of protons attached to an adjacent carbon. Thus, spin-spin splittings might be expected as the result of couplings between the individual protons at the methylene position of an ethyl group, as well as between the methylene and methyl protons. In practice, except for some special situations to be explained later, magnetic nuclei in equivalent chemical environments do not show spin-spin coupling. This is because equivalent protons do not absorb rf energy independently of one another. In spectroscopic terms, we can say that any transition which would lead to a splitting of the resonance of one proton of an equivalent group by the magnetic moment of another proton in the group would be "forbidden," since it would be a "singlet-triplet" transition. "Allowed" transitions involve absorption of energy by protons as a group, and no splittings result therefrom. With nuclei which are not completely equivalent, the type of transition forbidden for equivalent nuclei is allowed but reduced in probability—the closer the degree of equivalence, the lower the transition probability.[5]

It is instructive to consider the effect of coupling between two like nuclei as a function of the chemical shift between their resonances. When the chemical shift is large compared with J, the simple first-order treatment holds as described earlier and each of the resonances is split by the interaction between the nuclei into two lines of equal intensity, as shown in Fig. 3-9. The distance between the centers of the doublets is the chemical shift δH. Now, as the chemical shift decreases at constant J, a more complicated relation obtains between δH, J, the signal strengths, and the distances between the resonance lines. The splitting of the multiplets is still J, but the distance between the multiplet centers is no longer δH but $\sqrt{J^2 + \delta^2 H^2}$. The line intensities no longer remain equal—the center peaks get larger and the outer peaks smaller, so

$$\frac{\text{Intensity of inner lines}}{\text{Intensity of outer lines}} = \left(\frac{1+Q}{1-Q}\right)^2 \text{ where } Q = \frac{J}{\delta H + \sqrt{\delta^2 H^2 + J^2}}$$

[5] Cf. H. S. Gutowsky, *Ann. N.Y. Acad. Sci.*, **70**, 786 (1958); H. J. Bernstein, J. A. Pople, and W. G. Schneider, *Can. J. Chem.*, **35**, 65 (1957).

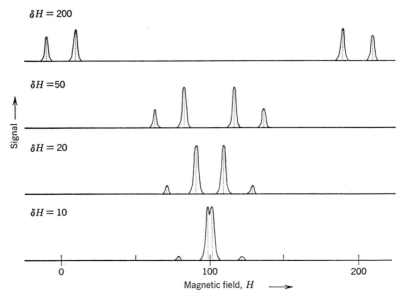

Fig. 3-9. Theoretical relation between line intensities and line positions as a function of chemical shift for two nonequivalent protons with a constant coupling J. For definiteness, J is taken to be 20 cps and δH is assumed to vary between 10 and 200 cps.

As δH continues to decrease, the outer lines get weaker and weaker, and, finally, when δH is smaller than J, the spectrum may appear to a casual observer as a closely spaced doublet. At very small δH values, the center lines coalesce and only one intense line is observed. The limiting case with $\delta H = 0$ corresponds to nuclei in equivalent chemical locations and no splitting is observed.

It should always be kept in mind that spectra involving spin-spin splittings will be distorted from the predictions of the simple first-order treatment and extra lines may even appear whenever the chemical shifts are small. Thus, the second-order spin-spin splitting displayed by ethanol at 40 Mc (Fig. 3-1) is much accentuated at lower frequencies. An excellent example of the striking effect of extreme changes of oscillator frequency on the appearance of NMR spectra has been provided by Muetterties and Phillips [6] for the ^{19}F resonances of chlorine trifluoride.

The chemical shifts between nuclei of different kinds, such as between hydrogen and fluorine, hydrogen and nitrogen, etc., are always very large, so that the above-mentioned complications do not arise except at very low field strengths.

[6] E. L. Muetterties and W. D. Phillips, *J. Am. Chem. Soc.*, **79**, 322 (1957).

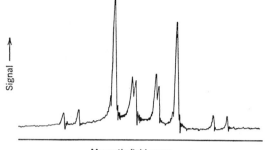

Fig. 3-10.   Proton NMR spectrum of 1,1-difluoroethylene at 40 Mc.

3-8.   Spin-Spin Couplings in Rigid Systems

Difficulties in interpretation of spin-spin couplings are very often encountered in more or less rigid complex molecules such as cyclic compounds. There are several reasons for expecting difficulties. First, as shown for styrene oxide, the protons of adjacent methylenes in a rigid system will generally have at least two spin-spin coupling constants which correspond to interactions between the various combinations of *cis* and *trans* protons. Second, *J* for protons on adjacent carbons shows a strong angular dependence and, as a result, the couplings in more or less rigid systems vary between zero and the values normally encountered for open-chain substances. Furthermore, it should be remembered that whenever *J* is large compared with the chemical shift, no splitting or chemical shift may be apparent in the spectrum. An example is cyclopentanone, which shows only a single proton resonance line.

A further and serious complication is introduced in rigid systems when chemically equivalent nuclei which are close enough to each other to be strongly coupled are also strongly coupled to other nuclei.[7] An excellent illustration is afforded by 1,1-difluoroethylene. Here, the first-order treatment predicts four resonance lines of equal intensity because each proton should be coupled to the two fluorines with different coupling constants, one fluorine being *cis* to a given proton and the other being *trans*. However, the observed spectrum shows ten lines (Fig. 3-10), and in the detailed mathematical treatment of spin-spin coupling for this molecule, both the fluorine-fluorine and proton-proton coupling make important contributions to the splitting. Generally, one will expect complications from couplings between formally equivalent nuclei wher-

[7] H. M. McConnell, A. D. McLean, and C. A. Reilly, *J. Chem. Phys.*, **23**, 1152 (1955).

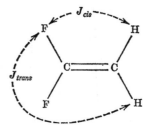

ever such nuclei are so located as to have different intramolecular coupling constants to other magnetic nuclei.

3-9.   Spin-Spin Splitting and Molecular Asymmetry

An interesting and unusual splitting is sometimes observed when a $-CH_2-Y$ group is attached to another carbon atom, carrying three different groups.[8]   An excellent example is methyl 2,3-dibromo-2-methylpropionate, the proton NMR spectrum of which is shown in Fig.

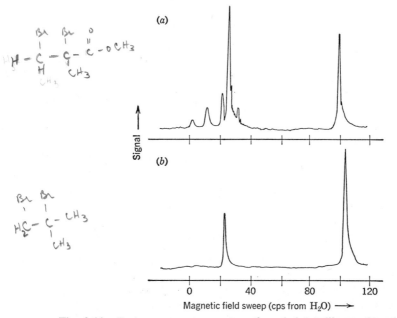

Fig. 3-11.   Proton resonance spectra of methyl 2,3-dibromo-2-methylpropionate (*a*) and 1,2-dibromo-2-methylpropane (*b*) at 40 Mc. (*Courtesy of the Journal of the American Chemical Society.*)

[8] P. M. Nair and J. D. Roberts, *J. Am. Chem. Soc.,* **79,** 4565 (1957).

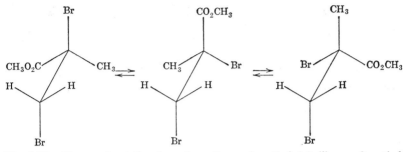

Fig. 3-12. Staggered rotational conformations of methyl 2,3-dibromo-2-methyl-propionate.

3-11. Besides the large three-proton resonance peaks of the ester and the α methyls there are four small peaks which fit the typical pattern of two nonequivalent protons, splitting each other with a coupling constant of about the same magnitude as the chemical shift. All chemical experience indicates that the rate of rotation of the groups with respect to one another around the 2,3-carbon-carbon single bond in this molecule should be reasonably rapid. However, there is good evidence that substituted ethanes of this type are more stable in the staggered conformations, as shown in Fig. 3-12.

In the present case, inspection of the various staggered conformations shows that the β-methylene hydrogens are not equivalently located in any one of them with respect to the groups attached to the carbon. Therefore, there must be at least some degree of nonequivalence of the β protons, and spin-spin splitting is consequently possible. At present, it is not known to what extent the relative residence times of the molecules in particular conformations are important in determining the degree of nonequivalence. If all the conformations had equal residence times and rapid rotation occurred, then each hydrogen would experience nearly the same average magnetic field. On the other hand, if the residence times were quite different, then the average magnetic field would be much like that of the most favored conformation and a larger degree of nonequivalence would be expected.

Ethanes with –CH$_2$–Y attached to –CX$_2$Y are not expected to show nonequivalent protons if rotation is rapid around the C–C bond. Thus, inspection of the possible staggered conformations for 1,2-dibromo-2-methylpropane (see Fig. 3-13) shows that the conformation with the bromines *trans* to one another has a plane of symmetry and the methylene hydrogens are thereby automatically equivalent. The other two conformations have nonequivalent protons, but since they are mirror images of each other, the protons will spend equal time in each.

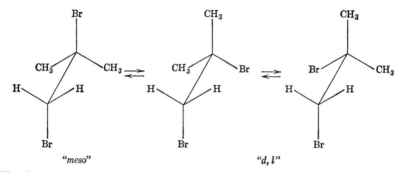

Fig. 3-13.   Staggered rotational conformations of 1,2-dibromo-2-methylpropane.

Therefore, if all the forms are interconverted rapidly, the two methylene protons will reside in identical average environments (cf. spectrum in Fig. 3-11). As will be seen later, slow rotation about the C–C bond in substances of this type will lead to more complex spectra because then the magnetic environments of the individual methylene protons are not identical in all the conformations.

The type of spin-spin splitting observed for methyl 2,3-bromo-2-methylpropionate appears to offer a new approach to detecting asymmetric centers in organic molecules without recourse to resolution into optical antipodes. Strictly, the method provides a test for a carbon with

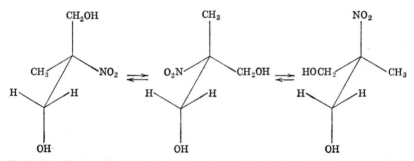

Fig. 3-14.   Staggered rotational conformations of 2-nitro-2-methyl-1,3-propanediol.

three different groups attached rather than a test for molecules which might be resolvable into optical antipodes. Thus, 2-nitro-2-methyl-1,3-propanediol is not capable of being resolved into optical antipodes but shows nonequivalent methylene protons because each methylene is attached to an asymmetric group (see Fig. 3-14). A comprehensive theoretical treatment of various types of asymmetric molecules has been made by Pople.[9]

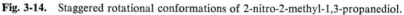

[9] J. A. Pople, *Molecular Physics,* **1,** 3 (1958).

CHAPTER 4

Nuclear Magnetic Resonance and Reaction Kinetics

4-1. Introduction. Proton Exchange in Water–Acetic Acid Mixtures

One of the most important applications of NMR spectroscopy is to the determination of kinetics of very fast reactions. Obviously, reaction kinetics could be followed by measuring rates of increase or decrease of resonance signals attributable to products or reactants. However, there is a very simple and much less conventional NMR method for determination of reaction rates which covers a range of rate constants and reaction types exceedingly difficult to measure in any other way.

As an introduction, we consider the NMR spectra of solutions of acetic acid and water. The spectra of the two separate substances are shown in Fig. 4-1, the carboxyl hydrogen of the acetic acid appearing

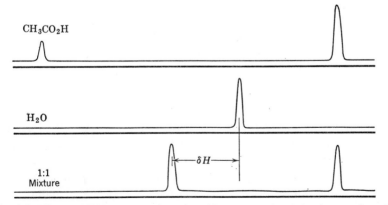

Fig. 4-1. Proton NMR spectra of acetic acid, water, and a 1:1 mixture of acetic acid and water.

61

at a very low field compared with water and the methyl group at a considerably higher field. When the substances are mixed, the spectrum might be expected to show three lines—one for the methyl group and two others corresponding to the two varieties of hydroxyl hydrogen. This prediction is buttressed by the knowledge that a variety of physical methods show that acetic acid in water is almost completely undissociated. Nonetheless, the simple expectation is not realized. Mixtures of acetic acid and water show only two lines—a methyl resonance and a hydroxyl resonance, the latter of which is intermediate between the normal positions of the carboxyl and water proton resonances. The position of this hydroxyl resonance depends on the concentrations, and in fact, a linear relationship has been demonstrated between the line position and the fraction of the hydroxyl protons in the form of acetic acid, as shown in Fig. 4-2.[1] This result is of considerable practical

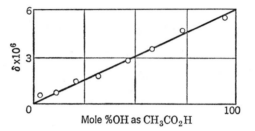

Fig. 4-2. Variation of position of hydroxyl resonance of acetic acid–water mixtures with composition. (*Courtesy of H. S. Gutowsky and the Journal of Chemical Physics.*)

interest in that it provides a means of analysis by virtue of measurements of line positions rather than of line areas. This type of NMR analysis is very advantageous where applicable because line positions are far more easily and accurately measured than the integrated resonance intensities.

Apart from applications to analysis, the occurrence of an average hydroxyl resonance line position from two chemically different species of hydroxyl protons is of considerable theoretical significance. The single hydroxyl line is a consequence of rapid chemical exchange between the hydroxyl hydrogens of acetic acid and water. It represents the hydroxyl protons in a time-averaged environment. Such a phenomenon is almost unthinkable to anyone brought up exclusively on visible and ultraviolet spectroscopy. Indeed, the Franck-Condon principle states that the transition time for an electronic excitation resulting from

[1] H. S. Gutowsky and A. Saika, *J. Chem. Phys.,* **21,** 1688 (1954).

the absorption of ultraviolet or visible electromagnetic radiation is short even compared with the rate at which the atoms vibrate in chemical bonds. However, in NMR spectroscopy, the transition times for excitation of the nuclei to higher energy magnetic states not only are long with respect to the rates of vibration of atoms in bonds but are also long with respect to rotations around single bonds and are even long with respect to rapid chemical reactions. In effect, the NMR spectrometer acts as a camera with a slow shutter speed and so records molecules in an average state taken over the relatively long periods of time required for the transitions of nuclei from one magnetic quantum state to another. The long transition times are associated with the fact that these magnetic transitions are induced by very low frequency radiations compared with the frequencies of ultraviolet and visible light.

The exchange of acetic acid and water hydroxyl protons appears always to be too fast to give anything but an average hydroxyl resonance line. With other substances, this is not always the case, and as will be seen later, separate hydroxyl absorptions can be obtained with mixtures of some hydroxyl compounds.

4-2.   Relationship between Resonance Line Shapes and Exchange Rates

In general, there will be a gradual change in the appearance of a resonance due to a magnetic nucleus in a particular chemical environment as the mean lifetime in that environment decreases. The changes which take place for the simple case where one type of nucleus undergoes exchange between environments A and B, in which on the average it spends equal lengths of time, are shown in Fig. 4-3. When the mean lifetime before exchange (τ_A or τ_B) is long compared with the transition time between the magnetic energy states, two separate sharp resonances $\delta_{AB}H$ apart are observed. When τ_A is short compared with the transition times, a single sharp resonance line at $\frac{1}{2}(\delta_A H + \delta_B H)$ is observed. An intermediate broad line is obtained when the mean lifetime before exchange is comparable with the transition time.

Gutowsky [2] has shown that the point at which the separate lines just coalesce corresponds to τ_A equal to $\sqrt{2}(\pi\delta_{AB}H)^{-1}$ sec when ($\delta_{AB}H$) is expressed in cycles per second or $2\sqrt{2}(\delta_{AB}H)^{-1}$ when $\delta_{AB}H$ is expressed in radians per second. The rate constant in either direction for $A \rightleftharpoons B$ will then be $1/\tau_A$. Expressions have also been derived for determining rate constants from changes in resonance line shape. In some instances, rate constants accurate to a few per cent have been reported.

[2] H. S. Gutowsky and C. H. Holm, *J. Chem. Phys.*, **25**, 1228 (1957).

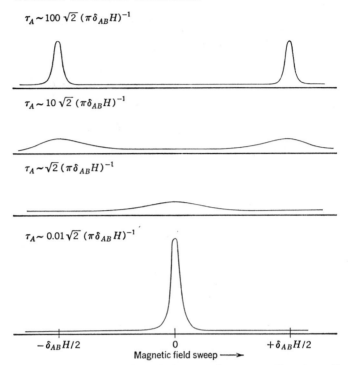

$$\tau_A \sim 100 \sqrt{2} \ (\pi \delta_{AB} H)^{-1}$$

$$\tau_A \sim 10 \sqrt{2} \ (\pi \delta_{AB} H)^{-1}$$

$$\tau_A \sim \sqrt{2} \ (\pi \delta_{AB} H)^{-1}$$

$$\tau_A \sim 0.01 \sqrt{2} \ (\pi \delta_{AB} H)^{-1}$$

$-\delta_{AB} H/2$ 0 $+\delta_{AB} H/2$

Magnetic field sweep ⟶

Fig. 4-3. Schematic representation of changes of resonance line shapes for protons exchanging between the nonequivalent magnetic environments A and B, where $[A]/[B] = 1$, as a function of exchange rate. (*Courtesy of H. S. Gutowsky and the Journal of Chemical Physics.*)

Since the easily measurable proton chemical shifts range from 5 to several hundred cycles per second, NMR spectroscopy is most useful for study of reactions which have mean lifetimes of the reacting species ranging between 0.1 and 0.0005 sec. We shall illustrate some of the potentialities of this method of determining reaction rates in a number of different kinds of kinetic processes.

4-3.   Proton Exchange in Ethanol-Water Mixtures

The work of Weinberg and Zimmerman [3] on the hydroxyl resonance in mixtures of ethanol and water is particularly interesting because it rounds out the picture of proton-exchange phenomena discussed earlier in connection with mixtures of acetic acid and water. We shall consider first mixtures of ethanol and water with relatively high water content.

[3] I. Weinberg and J. R. Zimmerman, *J. Chem. Phys.*, **23,** 748 (1955).

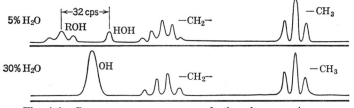

Fig. 4-4. Proton resonance spectra of ethanol-water mixtures.

The NMR spectrum (Fig. 4-4) of such a mixture with 30 per cent water shows three principal groups of resonance lines. The two groups at high fields arise from the ethyl protons as evidenced by the customary four-three pattern of spin-spin splitting. The large peak at low fields is the hydroxyl resonance and represents an average ethanol-water hydroxyl resulting from rapid exchange. As will be seen from Fig. 4-5, the position of this line is relatively insensitive to the composition of the mixture, down to about 25 per cent water. Now, the spectrum of ethanol containing only little water (and no acid or base or other substance which might catalyze exchange between the hydroxyls) is seen in Fig. 4-4 to have a quite different appearance from ethanol containing water in which exchange is rapid. At low fields, two groups of peaks appear instead of one. These represent the separate resonances of the water and the hydroxyl protons of ethanol in the mixture and can be easily distinguished by the fact that the alcohol hydroxyl resonance is split into three because of spin-spin coupling between the hydroxyl and methylene protons. The protons of the individual water molecules are, of course, equivalent, and their respective resonance is not split. In nonexchanging ethanol, the methylene resonance is seen to be substantially more complex than for exchanging ethanol. This is because the protons of the methylene group are coupled to both the methyl and the hydroxyl protons. If the coupling constants were equal, the methylene resonance

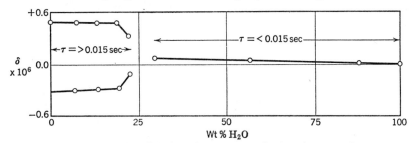

Fig. 4-5. Chemical shifts of hydroxyl resonance of ethanol-water mixtures as a function of composition. (*Courtesy of J. R. Zimmerman and the Journal of Chemical Physics.*)

would be expected to be split into five lines. This is approximately what is observed although complications are introduced because the respective J's are not exactly equal.

When rapid exchange sets in, the splitting caused by coupling between the hydroxyl and the methylene protons disappears somewhat sooner than the water and alcohol hydroxyl resonances merge to a single line. The splitting disappears with rapid exchange because as a given hydroxyl proton moves from alcohol to water to alcohol, etc., it experiences local fields produced by different combinations of the two spins of the methylene protons of different alcohol molecules. It does not stay on any one molecule long enough to give a resonance line corresponding to its particular spin combination. Instead, the exchanging proton acts as though it were experiencing an average of the possible CH_2 magnetic quantum numbers which is zero and, of course, would produce no splitting.

The reason that the spin-spin splittings between the hydroxyl and methylene protons disappear somewhat before the two hydroxyl lines merge into an average is because a splitting of about 5 cps will be averaged to zero by a process having a mean proton lifetime in the various states of less than 0.07 sec. On the other hand, two hydroxyl lines some 30 cps apart will be averaged by exchange only when the mean lifetime is less than about 0.015 sec. This type of situation where the same reaction process causes differently spaced lines to be averaged separately is particularly advantageous, since it allows determination of more than one rate constant as a function of temperature or concentration. Thus, two values of the rate of hydrogen exchange between water and alcohol as a function of concentration can be obtained by increasing the amount of water in the alcohol so as to wash out successively the hydroxyl-methylene spin-spin couplings and the separate hydroxyl resonances. Similarly, with a given alcohol-water composition, the rate of exchange could be ascertained at two different temperatures by determining the temperatures for separate averaging of the spin-spin couplings and the chemical shift, respectively.

The data presented in Fig. 4-5 show that the mean lifetime of a proton before exchange on the left of the transition point is greater than 0.015 sec, less than 0.015 sec on the right of the transition point, and about 0.015 sec in the neighborhood of the transition point. Acids and bases are powerful catalysts for the hydroxyl exchange, since alcohol samples which show the three-line hydroxyl resonance immediately give a single hydroxyl resonance when minute amounts of a strong acid or base are added. The kinetic order of acid or base in causing this exchange has not as yet been obtained accurately.

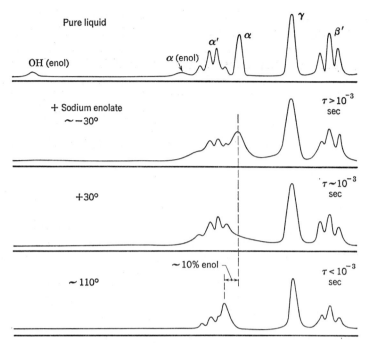

Fig. 4-6. Proton NMR spectra of ethyl acetoacetate at 40 Mc, pure liquid at room temperature and in the presence of some of the sodium enolate at various temperatures.

4-4. Ethyl Acetoacetate and Its Enol Form

Ethyl acetoacetate provides an interesting example of the use of NMR spectra for both a structural and kinetic analysis. The spectrum of the pure ester is shown in Fig. 4-6. The ethoxy group of the ester is easily identified by the typical four-three pattern of resonance lines. The other prominent resonances are due to the α and γ protons. These are approximately in the theoretical ratio 2:3 and appear in the anticipated order with respect to field strength. Thus, the protons on the α-carbon atom are adjacent to two electron-attracting carbonyl groups and give a resonance line at a considerably lower field than the protons

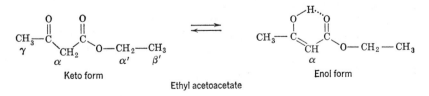

on the γ-carbon atom, which are adjacent to only one carbonyl group. At room temperature, ethyl acetoacetate contains about 10 per cent of the corresponding enol form. The presence of this material is shown by the NMR spectrum, there being a small band in the vinyl hydrogen region and a hydrogen-bonded hydroxyl proton resonance at very low fields. The strength of these bands agrees with the composition as established by the Kurt Meyer titration. Apparently, the γ-methyl and ethoxy resonances of the enol form are not separated enough from those of the keto form to make them easily distinguishable in the appropriate regions.

The detection of the separate resonances of the keto and enol forms shows that the enol and keto forms are not interconverted rapidly at room temperature, and this is in agreement with the observation that the enol and keto forms can be separated by "aseptic distillation" and separately preserved at low temperatures. The NMR spectrum of the equilibrium mixture of the ethyl acetoacetate tautomers at room temperature is markedly altered by the addition of a small amount of the sodium enolate (from dissolution of a small piece of sodium in the liquid), as shown in Fig. 4-6. The α-proton resonance of the keto form and vinyl and O–H resonances of the enol form disappear, and a new, rather broad band appears underneath the resonances of the α' hydrogens of the ethyl group. In the particular circumstances, exchange is occurring at an intermediate rate among the α-keto, vinyl-, and hydroxyl-enol hydrogens. Cooling the mixture slows down the rate of exchange and the α-hydrogen line reemerges, although somewhat broadened. On heating, the exchange rate is increased and a new rather sharp average line of the exchanging protons is produced.

Separate experiments have shown that the chemical shifts of the resonance lines of the keto form of ethyl acetoacetate are not substantially altered by raising the temperature. With this information, it is possible to calculate that about 10 per cent of the enol is present in the rapidly exchanging mixture at 110°, by virtue of the relative position of the average line with respect to the α-proton line of the keto form. The average consists of a small contribution of enol hydroxyl with a resonance line at a very low field, an equal-sized vinyl resonance at a much higher field, and a large contribution of α-keto hydrogens at a still higher field. Thus, the equilibrium composition of the tautomers of ethyl acetoacetate probably does not change markedly with temperature. A comparable analysis with acetylacetone indicates that with this liquid there is a greater temperature dependence for the position of its keto-enol equilibrium.

4-5.   Rates of Rotation Around –CO–N< Bonds of Amides

Of extraordinary interest and importance is the use of NMR methods to determine rates of rotation around single bonds.[4] The first observations of this kind were made with dimethylformamide.[5] The spectrum

Dimethylformamide

of dimethylformamide at room temperature is shown in Fig. 4-7. At low fields, there is a one-proton resonance which arises from the aldehyde-like hydrogen of the formyl group. The N-methyl proton resonances occur as two lines spaced about 10 cps apart at 40 Mc. The doublet methyl resonance might conceivably arise either from chemically different methyl groups or spin-spin coupling with the formyl proton. It will be noted from Fig. 4-7 that the formyl proton resonance is not split, so that the latter explanation is untenable. A chemical-shift difference

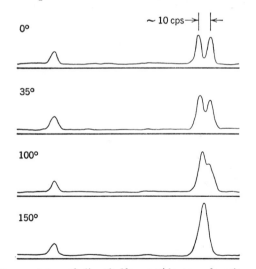

Fig. 4-7.   Proton spectrum of dimethylformamide as a function of temperature at 40 Mc.

[4] W. D. Phillips, *Ann. N.Y. Acad. Sci.,* **70,** 817 (1958).
[5] W. D. Phillips, *J. Chem. Phys.,* **23,** 1363 (1955).

has been established by the fact that at 30 Mc the two methyl peaks are only 7 cps apart. The knowledge that the separate methyl resonances arise from methyl groups in different chemical and magnetic environments forces the conclusion that there is restricted rotation around the –CO–N< bond of dimethylformamide. This is quite reasonable because resonance interaction between the carbonyl group and the unshared electron pair on nitrogen will tend to make all the atoms of the molecule lie in one plane, except for the protons on the methyl group. If the amide group is planar, one methyl group must be *cis* and the other *trans* to the carbonyl oxygen, and if rotation is slow about the –CO–N< bond, then the protons of each methyl will give a separate resonance line. On heating, the rate of rotation around the –CO–N< bond increases and finally the separate methyl resonances coalesce to a single line, as shown in Fig. 4-7. Considerable work has been done to determine the activation energy for rotation in dimethylformamide, and although the precision obtained by a given investigator is satisfactory, there are considerable discrepancies among the reported values.[2,6] This may possibly be due to effects of impurities.

Phillips [7] has made elegant use of the slowness of rotation around the –CO–N< bond of dimethylformamide to learn how the molecule accepts a proton in forming the conjugate acid. As shown in the following equation, the proton could add to either the oxygen or the nitrogen.

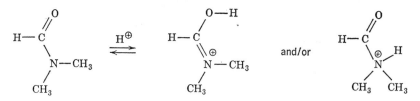

One could well argue that nitrogen is intrinsically more basic than oxygen, so that the nitrogen might be the favored position, even though addition of the proton to nitrogen would mean loss of resonance energy associated with the interaction of the nitrogen unshared electron pair with the carbonyl group. On the other hand, it could be argued that the amide oxygen would be more prone to accept a proton than usual for carbonyl oxygen because the resulting conjugate acid would be substantially stabilized by resonance involving the unshared electron pair on nitrogen.

[6] Research by J. N. Shoolery reported in *Varian Associates Tech. Bull.*, **2,** 7 (1957).

[7] Private communication from W. D. Phillips. Similar studies have been made by G. Fraenkel and C. Niemann, *Proc. Nat. Acad. Sci.*, **44,** 688 (1958).

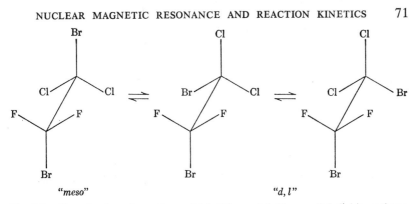

Fig. 4-8. Rotational conformations of 1,1-difluoro-1,2-dibromo-2,2-dichloroethane.

Phillips recognized that if the proton adds to nitrogen, this would destroy the double-bond character of the $-CO-N\!<$ bond and reduce the barrier to rotation to the very low value expected for a C–N single bond. On the other hand, if the proton adds to oxygen, then the amount of double-bond character in the $-CO-N\!<$ bond would be increased and rotation would be more difficult. Experimentally, it is observed that the rate of rotation around the single bond in dimethylformamide in strong acid solution is not increased compared with neutral solution, and therefore the added proton is preferentially attached to oxygen.

A number of interesting studies of restricted rotation in nitrites, N-nitrosoamines, and oximes have been reviewed by Phillips.[4]

4-6. Restricted Rotation in Ethane Derivatives

In favorable circumstances, the rates of rotation around C–C bonds in ethane derivatives can be shown by NMR methods to be slow.[4,8] An excellent example is afforded by the behavior of 1,1-difluoro-1,2-dibromo-2,2-dichloroethane.[8] The ^{19}F nuclear resonance spectrum of this substance at room temperature shows a single sharp line. Inspection of the possible rotational conformations (Fig. 4-8) shows that a single ^{19}F line is to be expected either as a result of averaging of the fluorines by rapid rotation or else, if rotation is slow, because the substance is "locked into" the *"meso"* conformation (I) with the 1,2-bromines *trans* to one another and the fluorines equivalently located. The other possible staggered conformations are seen to be a *"d,l"* pair (II and III) and to have nonequivalent fluorines. Rapid equilibrium of these two rotational isomers would average the fluorine spectrum to a single line because, as one isomer goes to the other, the fluorines exchange magnetic environ-

[8] P. M. Nair and J. D. Roberts, *J. Am. Chem. Soc.,* **79,** 4565 (1957).

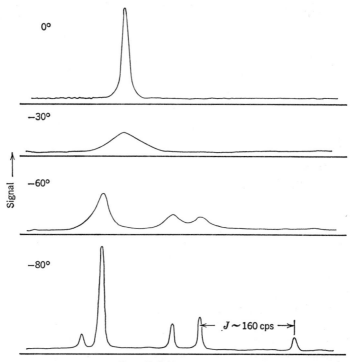

Fig. 4-9. Fluorine resonance spectrum of 1,1-difluoro-1,2-dibromo-2,2-dichloro-ethane at 40 Mc as a function of temperature.

ments. Therefore, the rotational isomers must be rapidly equilibrated or else the substance must exist predominantly in a symmetrical form in order that only a single resonance line be obtained.

The ^{19}F spectrum of 1,1-difluoro-1,2-dibromo-2,2-dichloroethane is quite temperature dependent, as is shown in Fig. 4-9. At $-30°$, the single line is seen to broaden substantially; at $-60°$, new lines commence to appear; and at $-80°$, five sharp lines are observed. These lines can be easily identified by their spin-spin coupling patterns. Four of the lines represent the spectra of the d,l pair II and III, which have non-equivalent fluorines, so that the fluorine resonances are shifted from one another and the concomitant spin-spin interactions give a quartet of lines with the outer lines being weakened by virtue of J being comparable with δH.

Since the rotational isomers II and III are mirror images, they will give identical spectra, and the symmetrical four-line pattern in Fig. 4-9 represents the contribution of this pair. The large single sharp resonance

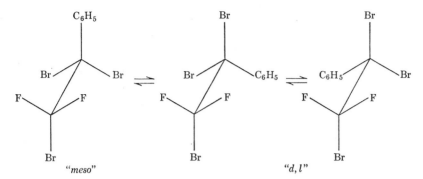

Fig. 4-10.   Rotational conformations of 1,1-difluoro-1,2,2-tribromo-2-phenylethane.

is due to the symmetrical *"meso"* rotational isomer with equivalent fluorines. At $-80°$, the rate of interconversion of these isomers must be much less than 200 times per second. On a purely statistical basis, the ratio of I to the isomers II and III should be 1:2. However, a rough analysis of the mixture at $-80°$ by measuring the ratios of the signal intensities indicates that the composition is actually close to 1.4:1. This ratio is quite reasonable, since the conformation with two bromines *trans* to each other is expected to be sterically favored.

It is possible that valuable information as to relative steric sizes of groups will be obtainable through NMR studies of rotational isomer populations. An excellent example is afforded by 1,1-difluoro-1,2,2-tribromo-2-phenylethane. The ^{19}F spectrum of this substance at room temperature shows a single line, while at $-80°$ there are five lines as expected from a "freezing out" of the rotational isomers. The *"meso"* isomer of 1,1-difluoro-1,2,2-tribromo-2-phenylethane has phenyl *trans* to bromine, and this would be expected to be the favorable conformation if phenyl were sterically larger than bromine as far as influencing the populations of the various configurations goes (see Fig. 4-10). However, the NMR spectrum (Fig. 4-11) shows that the *meso* isomer is actually present in far smaller concentration than the *d,l* pair, and in this case, we conclude that bromine acts as though it were larger than

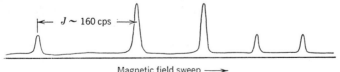

Fig. 4-11.   Fluorine resonance spectrum of 1,1-difluoro-1,2,2-tribromo-2-phenyl-ethane at 40 Mc and $-80°$.

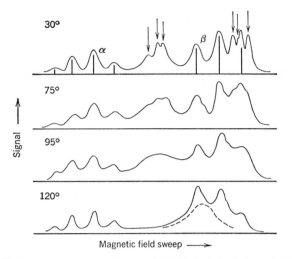

Fig. 4-12. Proton resonance spectrum of N-ethylethylenimine at 40 Mc as a function of temperature. Heavy vertical lines mark the characteristic resonances of the ethyl group, while vertical arrows indicate resonances of ring protons. (*Courtesy of the Journal of the American Chemical Society.*)

phenyl. Extensions of this type of experiment can clearly provide much information with regard to rotation about single bonds which is not easily available in any other way.

4-7.   Nitrogen Inversion Frequencies of Cyclic Imines

Another interesting process which can be studied by NMR spectroscopy is the rate of inversion of nonplanar nitrogen carrying substituent groups. Ammonia has long been known from its rf spectrum to undergo inversion extremely rapidly. The corresponding inversion frequencies of various alkyl- and aryl-substituted amines have not been determined, but a variety of experiments have failed to provide optically active isomers of trisubstituted amines that are asymmetric solely because of the configuration at the nitrogen atom, presumably because inversion is too rapid. In 1940, Kincaid and Henriques [9] published calculations which indicated that the rates of inversion of substituted nitrogen compounds would be much smaller if two of the substituents on nitrogen were connected together so as to form a three-membered N–C–C ring. However, prior and subsequent attempts to resolve such substituted ethylenimine derivatives into optically active forms were unsuccessful.

[9] J. F. Kincaid and F. C. Henriques, Jr., *J. Am. Chem. Soc.,* **62,** 1474 (1940).

Nonetheless, the predictions of Kincaid and Henriques have been confirmed through the NMR spectra of cyclic imines.[10]

The proton resonance spectrum of N-ethylethylenimine at various temperatures is shown in Fig. 4-12. At room temperature, the typical three-four line pattern of the N-ethyl group is easily recognized and there remain two groups of lines to be assigned which arise from the ring protons. Models of N-ethylethylenimine show that, if the nitrogen is not planar, one would expect two kinds of ring protons—ones which are *cis* to the ethyl group and ones which are *trans* to the ethyl group.

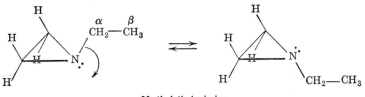

N-ethylethylenimine

These will be in different magnetic environments and can account for the two observed peaks about 30 cps apart. Since nitrogen inversion results in exchange of the environments of the ring protons, the mean lifetime of an ethylenimine molecule before inversion occurs must be much longer than 0.015 sec if the *cis-* and *trans*-ring protons are to give separate sharp resonances. At higher temperatures, the inversion rate increases, and, finally, at 120°, the two ring-hydrogen resonances coalesce to a single line. The intermediate temperature is about 110°, and at this point the mean lifetime of the molecule before inversion is about 0.015 sec.

Effects of substituents on the inversion rates of cyclic imines have been studied by the NMR method, and it has been found that bulky groups either on the ring or on the nitrogen tend to increase the inversion rates, presumably by destabilizing the separate nonplanar configurations relative to the transition state. Unsaturated groups connected to either the ring or the nitrogen of ethylenimine cause the inversion rates to increase markedly. Presumably, with such substituents, the planar transition state is stabilized relative to the nonplanar ground state by resonance interaction between the unshared pair of electrons on nitrogen and the unsaturated centers. N-Ethylallenimine provides an excellent example of this type of behavior and the temperature dependence of its NMR spectrum is shown in Fig. 4-13.

[10] A. T. Bottini and J. D. Roberts, *J. Am. Chem. Soc.,* **78,** 5126 (1956), and **80,** 5203 (1958).

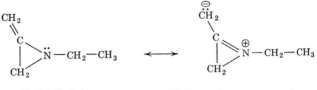

N-ethylallenimine

Solvents like water or alcohol which can form hydrogen bonds to the unshared electron pairs of ethylenimines substantially reduce the imine inversion frequencies. Presumably, the hydrogen bonds stabilize the nonplanar configuration by tending to anchor the unshared electron pairs on nitrogen.

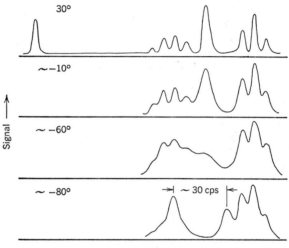

Fig. 4-13. Proton resonance spectrum of N-ethylallenimine at 40 Mc as a function of temperature. The ring proton resonances coalesce at about −70° at which temperature the lifetime before inversion is approximately 0.015 sec. Vinyl proton resonance shown at low fields at 30° does not change perceptibly with temperature. (*Courtesy of the Journal of the American Chemical Society.*)

4-8.   Proton Exchange in Ammonia and Ammonium Ions

A number of interesting exchange experiments of other kinds have been done with nitrogen compounds. Only one sharp proton resonance has been observed [11,12] for ammonia-water mixtures, as would be anticipated for a rapidly exchanging system. Extremely anhydrous liquid ammonia or gaseous ammonia gives a triplet resonance pattern with

[11] R. A. Ogg, Jr., *J. Chem. Phys.*, **22**, 560 (1954).
[12] H. S. Gutowsky and S. Fujiwara, *J. Chem. Phys.*, **22**, 1782 (1954).

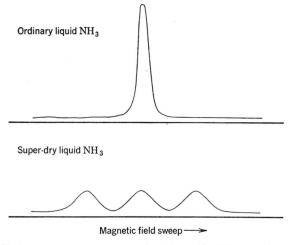

Fig. 4-14. Proton resonance spectrum of ordinary liquid ammonia and superdry ammonia as prepared by Ogg.[11]

all of the peaks being the same height (see Fig. 4-14).[11] This pattern arises from spin-spin coupling between the protons and the ^{14}N nucleus, which has a spin of 1 and hence the magnetic quantum numbers $+1$, 0, -1, which are equally probable. The line at the lowest field represents the proton resonance absorption of those ammonia molecules having nitrogen with a magnetic quantum number $+1$, while the center and high-field lines correspond to the nitrogen nuclei with magnetic quantum numbers 0 and -1, respectively.

In the presence of water or minute amounts of amide ion, exchange of hydrogens between ammonia molecules is extremely rapid, so that the spin-spin splitting is washed out when the mean lifetime of a proton on any given nitrogen is substantially less than 0.007 sec. In aqueous solution, exchange is so rapid between ammonia and water molecules that separate O–H and N–H resonances are not obtained and only a single average proton resonance is obtained. Similar results are obtained with ammonium nitrate solutions in water containing enough additional ammonia to make the solution nearly neutral. Under these circumstances, ammonium ions, ammonia, and water exchange protons with one another sufficiently rapidly to give only a single line. A startling change takes place on the acidification of such solutions with nitric acid.[13] As is seen in Fig. 4-15, a triplet pattern appears which corresponds to the three possible spin orientations of the ^{14}N nuclei and there is an additional large single proton resonance, that of water. This result

[13] R. A. Ogg, Jr., *Discussions Faraday Soc.*, 215 (1954).

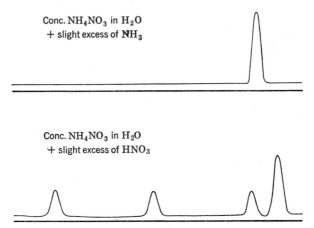

Fig. 4-15. Proton resonance spectra of concentrated solutions of ammonium nitrate in water containing either a slight excess of ammonia or nitric acid. The splitting of the N–H resonances in the lower spectrum persists even to 100°.

proves that water is singularly ineffective in removing protons from ammonium ions while ammonia is extremely effective. Similar observations [14] have been made for methylammonium ion, the spectrum of which in acidic solution is shown in Fig. 4-16. The broad N–H reso-

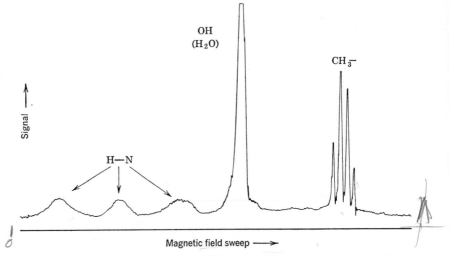

Fig. 4-16. Proton spectrum of an acidified methylammonium chloride solution at 40 Mc. The splitting of the methyl resonance into four lines results from spin-spin interaction with the three ammonium protons.

[14] J. D. Roberts, *J. Am. Chem. Soc.,* **78,** 4495 (1956).

nances which contrast to the sharp lines observed for ammonium ion result from quadrupole effects as will be discussed later and not from intermediate proton exchange rates, because further addition of acid does not cause the lines to sharpen. It is possible to obtain the exchange-rate constants by observations of line-shape changes with temperature or pH. The kinetics and mechanisms of such processes have been studied in detail by Grunwald and coworkers.[15]

[15] E. Grunwald, A. Loewenstein, and S. Meiboom, *J. Chem. Phys.,* **27,** 630 (1957).

CHAPTER 5

Nuclear Quadrupole Relaxation Effects. Double Resonance

5-1. Proton Resonance Line Broadening by ^{14}N

The broad N–H lines observed for the proton resonance spectrum (Fig. 4-16) of methylammonium ion in acid solution are worthy of special mention. Similar N–H resonances have been noted for quite a variety of substances provided the protons are not undergoing rapid exchange.[1] Pyrrolidine hydrochloride affords a particularly striking ex-

Pyrrolidine
hydrochloride

ample of this behavior. The methylene protons of pyrrolidine hydrochloride in a solution containing a slight excess of pyrrolidine (Fig. 5-1) show reasonably normal spin-spin couplings. Under these circumstances, the N–H proton and the water proton resonances are averaged. Acidification of the pyrrolidine hydrochloride solution effectively stops exchange but results in broad N–H resonances which, as mentioned before in connection with methylammonium ion, could conceivably be due to intermediate proton exchange rates with the water. However, this interpretation is ruled out by virtue of the fact that Fig. 5-1 shows the N–H protons to be coupled to the α-methylene protons. If there were intermediate exchange rates, then one would expect that the N–H:C–H splittings would be washed out before the N–H resonances themselves were appreciably broadened.

[1] J. D. Roberts, *J. Am. Chem. Soc.*, **78**, 4495 (1956).

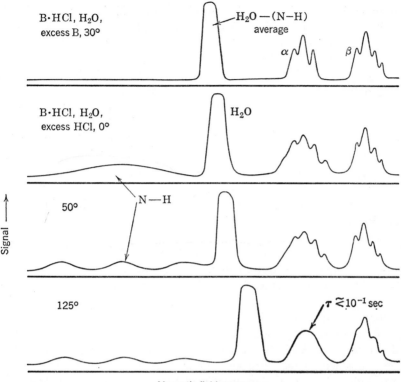

Fig. 5-1. Proton NMR spectrum of pyrrolidine hydrochloride (B·HCl) in basic and acidic solutions. Note increase in splitting of α-methylene proton resonances in acid solution. This extra splitting, which persists to above 50°, arises from magnetic interactions with the ammonium protons and shows that exchange between the ammonium and water protons is quite slow at 50° or less.

Besides being broad, the N–H resonances of substituted ammonium ions behave anomalously with temperature. Thus, lowering the temperature causes the three-line pattern to disappear and be replaced by a very broad single N–H resonance.[1] On the other hand, raising the temperature tends to sharpen the triplet pattern, although, in any case, the lines are much broader than for the resonances of the protons of ammonium ion itself.

N.B.

5-2.   Nuclear Quadrupoles and Quadrupole-induced Relaxation

The above observations are the result of changes in the magnetic quantum numbers of the ^{14}N nuclei in substituted ammonium ions through interaction of the ^{14}N electric quadrupoles with surrounding asymmetrical electric fields. The mechanism for this is not so formidable as it might sound. In the first place, we noted earlier (pages 6 and 7) that nuclei with spins I of 0 or $\frac{1}{2}$ act as though their charges were distributed over a spherical surface. With those nuclei like ^{14}N having $I > \frac{1}{2}$, however, the nuclear charge appears to be distributed over an ellipsoidal surface, and such nuclei act like electric quadrupoles. The symmetry axis of a nuclear quadrupole is collinear with the magnetic and angular momentum vectors of the nucleus. Now, consider a ^{14}N nuclear quadrupole such as the nitrogen of pyrrolidinium ion surrounded by a cloud of valence electrons which is not spherically symmetrical. The rapid tumbling motions of the ion in solution will cause a time-variable electric torque to be exerted on the quadrupole which will tend to shift the quadrupole orientation. Changes in the orientation of the quadrupole also result in changes in the direction of the magnetic vector of the nucleus. A relaxation mechanism is thereby provided for the ^{14}N nuclear magnet (see Fig. 5-2). Now, if the nitrogen nucleus of an ^{14}N–H compound is caused to flip back and forth among its several possible magnetic quantum states, the attached proton will "see" more or less of an average of three orientations of the nitrogen nucleus depending on the rate of flipping.

In solutions of pyrrolidinium ion at room temperature, relaxation of the nitrogen nucleus takes place at a rate such as to render the hydrogens attached to the nitrogen somewhat confused as to the ^{14}N spin orientation. This results in broadened N–H proton resonance lines. At room temperature, the N–H line is intermediate between a singlet and triplet absorption, so that the mean lifetime of the nitrogen with a given magnetic quantum number is on the order of the reciprocal of $\pi\sqrt{2}/2$ times the triplet line separation, or about 0.009 sec. When the temperature is raised, the increased rate of tumbling of the molecules apparently results in less efficient nitrogen relaxation and the proton resonance goes to a broad triplet. When the temperature is lowered, the decreased tumbling rate allows for rather more efficient nitrogen

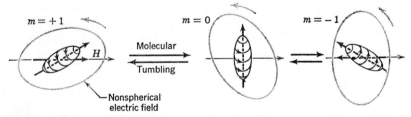

Fig. 5-2. Interaction of a nuclear quadrupole with an asymmetrical electrical field in a tumbling molecule. Horizontal line shows direction of applied magnetic field.

relaxation and the triplet proton resonance lines coalesce to a broad singlet. Only a sharp triplet absorption is observed for nonexchanging ammonium ions because in these ions the electric field around the nucleus is spherically symmetrical and quadrupole-induced relaxation is not effective.

5-3. Proton N–H Resonance of Pyrrole. Double Resonance

Broadening of N–H proton resonance lines by quadrupole-induced relaxation has been observed with a number of types of nitrogen com-

Pyrrole

pounds. A particularly striking example is afforded by pyrrole. The NMR spectrum of pyrrole at room temperature shows no N–H line on casual inspection (see Fig. 5-3). The principal observed peaks are those

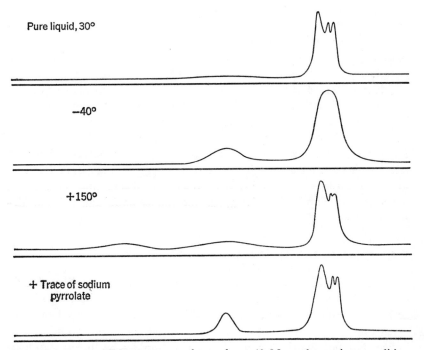

Pure liquid, 30°

−40°

+150°

+ Trace of sodium pyrrolate

Fig. 5-3. Proton NMR spectrum of pyrrole at 40 Mc under various conditions with only fair resolution.

of the C–H protons. However, very careful inspection of the spectrum shows a very broad peak to the low-field side of the C–H resonances, which rises only slightly above the base line. Apparently, the ^{14}N nucleus in pyrrole is undergoing relaxation at just the right rate to cause the protons attached to it to give the broadest possible line intermediate between the singlet and triplet patterns.

Any process which causes the N–H protons to "see" either a more slowly or more rapidly moving sequence of nitrogen magnetic quantum states will sharpen the resonance lines to give the triplet or singlet lines, respectively. As is seen in Fig. 5-3, this may be achieved by raising or lowering the temperature so as to change the rates of tumbling of the molecules and thus influence the effectiveness of the quadrupole relaxation of the nitrogen nucleus. As with pyrrolidine hydrochloride, lowering the temperature gives a sharpened single resonance, while raising the temperature causes a triplet pattern to appear. A given N–H proton of pyrrole can be exposed to a more rapid sequence of nitrogen magnetic quantum states by addition of potassium pyrrolate, which induces intermolecular proton exchange. As expected, exchange causes the N–H resonance line to sharpen.

By far the most elegant procedure for eliminating the magnetic relaxation effects of the ^{14}N nucleus is the "double-resonance" or "spin-decoupling" technique. As applied by Shoolery [2] to pyrrole, this involves observing the proton spectrum in the normal way while subjecting the sample to a powerful rf field at the ^{14}N resonance frequency (2.9 Mc at 9400 gauss). The proton signal is detected with a narrow-bandwidth receiver, so that there is no pickup of the second oscillator frequency. The rf input at the ^{14}N frequency causes the nitrogen nuclei to change their magnetic quantum numbers rather more rapidly than is possible for quadrupole-induced relaxation alone. As a result, each N–H proton sees its nitrogen nucleus with the magnetic quantum numbers effectively averaged to zero and thus gives a sharpened N–H resonance (Fig. 5-4). Several other applications of double-resonance technique will be described in Sec. 5-5.

5-4.   Quadrupole-induced Relaxation with Other Nuclei

All nuclei which have a spin of greater than $\frac{1}{2}$ act like electric quadrupoles and undergo more or less efficient relaxation through interactions with surrounding dissymmetric electric fields produced by their valence electrons. Most of the halogen nuclei (chlorine, bromine, and iodine, but not fluorine) are relaxed very rapidly by the quadrupole-

---

[2] Private communication from J. N. Shoolery.

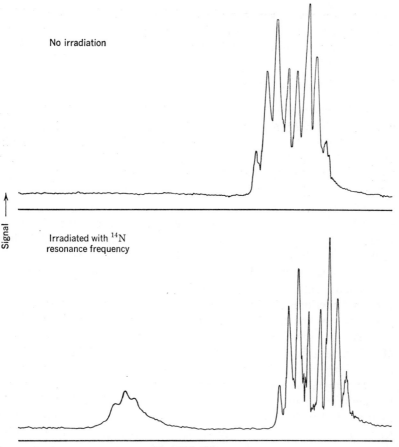

Fig. 5-4. Proton NMR spectrum of pyrrole at 40 Mc and 9,400 gauss with and without sample subjected to a powerful rf field at 2.9 Mc which is the ^{14}N-resonance frequency at 9,400 gauss. The triplet splitting of the N–H absorption in the lower spectrum is a consequence of magnetic interactions between the N–H and α-ring protons. This spectrum was taken under higher resolution than those of Fig. 5-3. (*Courtesy of James N. Shoolery and Varian Associates.*)

electric field interactions. As a result, even though these nuclei have considerable magnetic moments, they do not normally cause spin-spin splitting as might be expected for proton-halogen coupling in compounds like methyl chloride, bromide, or iodide, because rapid relaxation averages the magnetic effects of the halogens to zero. ^{14}N is notorious for its tendency to relax at intermediate rates when unsymmetrically substituted and this causes broadening of N–H proton resonance signals. However, with a number of amino compounds, such as ethylamine, sharp proton resonances are observed for the N–H protons. This is surely a consequence of rapid intermolecular exchange between the N–H protons rather than rapid quadrupole-electric field relaxation.

5-5. Applications of Double Resonance

The double-resonance technique described in Sec. 5-3 has important uses in analysis of complex spin-spin coupling patterns when two or more varieties of nuclei with different precession frequencies are involved. Valuable information for the analysis of the NMR spectra of boron hydrides has been obtained by Shoolery [3] by collapsing of spin-spin multiplets due to ^{10}B and ^{11}B while observing proton resonances.

Double resonance has also been utilized to aid in direct determinations of the H–F spin couplings in fluorobenzene.[4] With ordinary fluorobenzene, spin-spin splitting makes the spectrum complex and difficult to analyze. In principle, the problem of determining coupling constants for interactions between the fluorine and the hydrogens at the $o, m,$ and p positions can be greatly simplified through study of splittings in various deuterium-substituted fluorobenzenes. Thus, to obtain the coupling between the fluorine and meta hydrogens, 2,4,6-trideuterofluorobenzene can be employed. However, the proton spectrum (Fig. 5-5a) of this molecule is rendered more complex than might otherwise be expected because of F–D and H–D couplings which are at least as difficult to unravel as the spectrum of ordinary fluorobenzene. However, the double-resonance technique permits averaging of the deuterium spins to zero, so that the residual clean doublet observed in the proton spectrum (Fig. 5-5b) is due only to 1,3-proton-fluorine coupling with J equal to 5.8 cps. A similar study of 2,3,5,6-tetradeuterofluorobenzene shows that coupling between fluorine and para protons is negligible.

Double resonance would be extremely valuable in the analysis of spin-spin couplings in compounds with interacting nuclei of the same type. For example, one might use a suitable oscillator to "stir up" the methylene protons of ethanol while observing the methyl protons at another precession frequency. In such circumstances, the methyl resonance would be averaged to a single line and it would then be known that the splitting ordinarily observed arises from the various possible combinations of magnetic quantum numbers of the methylene protons. Unfortunately, this type of double resonance is not experimentally easy because it is necessary to use a considerably higher rf power level to

---

[3] J. N. Shoolery, *Discussions Faraday Soc.*, 215 (1955); R. Schaeffer, J. N. Shoolery, and R. Jones, *J. Am. Chem. Soc.*, **79**, 4606 (1957).

[4] B. Bak, J. N. Shoolery, and G. A. Williams, III, *J. Mol. Spectroscopy,* in press.

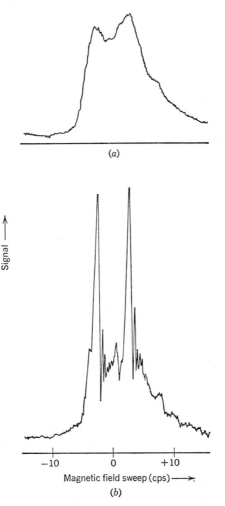

Fig. 5-5. Proton resonance spectra of 2,4,6-trideuterofluorobenzene: (*a*) normal spectrum, (*b*) irradiated with deuterium resonance frequency, 6.1 Mc at 9,400 gauss. (*Courtesy of James N. Shoolery and Varian Associates.*)

stir up one variety of proton than is necessary or desirable for the observation of the resonance of another variety of proton. As a result, one needs a receiving arrangement with high discriminating power to distinguish between the decoupling frequency and the observing frequency which may differ only by 100 cps at 40 Mc. Successful experiments of this type have been reported by Anderson,[5] but the method cannot yet be regarded as being applicable to routine work.

[5] W. A. Anderson, *Phys. Rev.,* **102,** 151 (1956).

APPENDIX A

The Bloch Equations

The following simplified treatment of Bloch's [1] derivation of equations which define nuclear resonance line shapes is intended primarily to show the difference between nuclear resonance absorption and dispersion modes. As such, it should make clear the reasons for certain internal adjustments in the NMR probe which influence the shape of the signal curves.

We consider first the magnetic vector **M** which is the resultant sum of the magnetic vectors of the individual nuclei per unit volume. For the present purposes, we shall not have **M** collinear with any of the axes but assume it to have components along the axes of M_x, M_y, and M_z, as shown in Fig. A-1. The Z axis (here the vertical direction) will be taken along the magnetic field axis, while the X axis will coincide with the axis of the oscillator coil, and the Y axis will coincide with the axis of the receiver coil. The vector **M** is subjected to the oscillator field, which as before (page 15) will be resolved into two vectors of length H_1 rotating at angular velocities ω and in opposite directions in the X, Y plane with phase relationships such as to give no net field along Y. These contrarotating fields have components in the X and Y directions which are given by the equations

Clockwise rotation	Counterclockwise rotation
$H_x = H_1 \cos \omega t$	$H_x = H_1 \cos \omega t$
$H_y = -H_1 \sin \omega t$	$H_y = H_1 \sin \omega t$

The sum of these fields gives $H_x = 2H_1 \cos \omega t$ and $H_y = 0$. We shall assume henceforth that only one of these rotating fields, here arbitrarily taken to have clockwise rotation, will influence the nuclei to change their m values (cf. Sec. 1-4).

[1] F. Bloch, *Phys. Rev.,* **70**, 460 (1946).

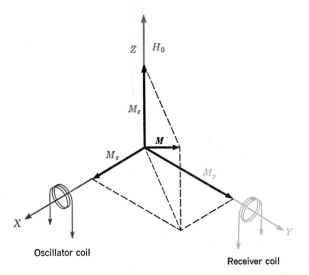

Fig. A-1. Cartesian coordinate system for consideration of interaction of oscillator field with vector of nuclear magnets. Note that the Z axis is taken vertically in contrast to the convention used in Chap. 1.

Let us consider possible changes of M_z. In the first place, M_z will tend to increase and approach its equilibrium value M_0 by relaxation with the time constant T_1 so that, if nothing else were to happen, we would write

$$\frac{dM_z}{dt} = \frac{1}{T_1} (M_0 - M_z)$$

At the same time, M_z will change by the action of H_x and H_y on the vectors M_y and M_x, respectively. Consider first the action of H_x on M_y.

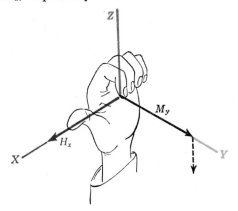

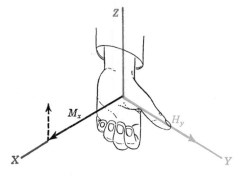

Using a "left-hand rule," we can say that H_x will cause the magnetization vector along Y to move downward and thus increase M_z in the negative direction. This contribution to M_z will be given by

$$\frac{dM_z}{dt} = -\gamma M_y H_x$$

Through proper choice of units the proportionality constant γ can have the same numerical value as the nuclear gyromagnetic ratio because, in effect, H_x causes the components of the individual nuclear vectors (which add to give the Y magnetization) to tend to precess around the X axis with an angular velocity of γH_x. H_y produces a similar contribution with opposite sign to M_z by making the M_x vector tip. We may then write

$$\frac{dM_z}{dt} = \frac{1}{T_1}(M_0 - M_z) - \gamma M_y H_x + \gamma M_x H_y$$

For the clockwise-rotating H_1, substitution for H_x and H_y gives

$$\frac{dM_z}{dt} = \frac{1}{T_1}(M_0 - M_z) - \gamma(M_y H_1 \cos \omega t + M_x H_1 \sin \omega t)$$

Operating in the same way on M_x, we have

$$\frac{dM_x}{dt} = \gamma M_y H_0 - \gamma M_z H_y - \frac{M_x}{T_2}$$

where the first and second terms on the right correspond to the tipping of M_y by H_0 and M_z by H_y, respectively. The last term represents the first-order decay of M_x with the time constant T_2. Similar treatment of M_y and substitution of the values for H_x and H_y as a function of time afford the following equations, which in combination with the expression above for dM_z/dt are called the Bloch equations:

$$\frac{dM_x}{dt} = \gamma M_y H_0 + \gamma M_z H_1 \sin \omega t - \frac{M_x}{T_2}$$

$$\frac{dM_y}{dt} = -\gamma M_x H_0 + \gamma M_z H_1 \cos \omega t - \frac{M_y}{T_2}$$

Consider now the projection of **M** on the X, Y plane M_{xy}. Movement of M_{xy} so as to produce a change in M_y will cause a current to be induced in the receiver coil mounted with its axis along Y. It is particularly useful to consider M_{xy} to be made up of two magnetic components u and v which are in phase with H_1 and 90° out of phase with H_1, respectively, so that $M_{xy} = u + iv$. The components u and v can be defined by the equations

$$u = M_x \cos \omega t - M_y \sin \omega t$$
$$v = -(M_x \sin \omega t + M_y \cos \omega t)$$

and thence, in combination with the Bloch equations (and remembering that $\gamma H_0 = \omega_0$),

$$\frac{du}{dt} = -(\omega_0 - \omega)v - \frac{u}{T_2}$$

$$\frac{dv}{dt} = (\omega_0 - \omega)u - \frac{v}{T_2} - \gamma H_1 M_z$$

$$\frac{dM_z}{dt} = \frac{(M_0 - M_z)}{T_1} + \gamma H_1 v$$

The last equation is particularly significant, since it shows that the energy absorbed by the nuclei through changes in their magnetic quantum numbers with respect to H_0 (cf. Sec. 1-4) is a function of $-v$ and not of u. This means that one must measure $-v$ if one desires a measure of the energy absorbed by the nuclei as a function of H_0 at constant H_1. However, the receiver responds to M_y which is made up of both u and v, and our problem will be to show how a measure of v can be obtained independently of u.

We shall be particularly interested in the case where H_0 is held constant and a steady signal is picked up in the receiver such as if the magnetic field sweep were stopped on the side or peak of a resonance signal. In these circumstances, M_{xy} has a constant length and rotates around the Z axis at the frequency ω. The steady-state condition requires that

$$\frac{du}{dt} = \frac{dv}{dt} = \frac{dM_z}{dt} = 0$$

With these conditions, it is easy to show that

$$u = -T_2(\omega_0 - \omega)v$$

($\omega_0 - \omega$ is a measure of how far we are off the peak of resonance.)

$$v = -\frac{\gamma T_2 H_1 M_z}{1 + T_2{}^2(\omega_0 - \omega)^2}$$

$$M_z = M_0 \frac{1 + T_2^2(\omega_0 - \omega)^2}{1 + T_2^2(\omega_0 - \omega)^2 + \gamma^2 H_1^2 T_1 T_2}$$

Substituting the equation for M_z into that for v gives

$$v = -\frac{\gamma H_1 M_0 T_2}{1 + T_2^2 (\omega_0 - \omega)^2 + \gamma^2 H_1^2 T_1 T_2} \tag{1}$$

and thence we may derive

$$u = \frac{\gamma H_1 (\omega_0 - \omega) T_2^2 M_0}{1 + T_2^2 (\omega_0 - \omega)^2 + \gamma^2 H_1^2 T_1 T_2} \tag{2}$$

The above final equations for u and v contain only observable quantities except for M_0, which can be computed according to the Boltzmann distribution law (page 9).

Assuming steady values for u, v, and M_z for some set of values of H_0, H_1, M_0, T_1, and T_2, we are interested in M_{xy} or actually M_y, which determines the signal strength. In Fig. A-2, we see the variation of the field due to M_y and H_x as a function of ωt for the case that $\omega = \omega_0$ so that from Eq. (2) above we see that $u = 0$. In this situation, $M_{xy} = iv$, and from the definition of v, the vector M_{xy} must be 90° out

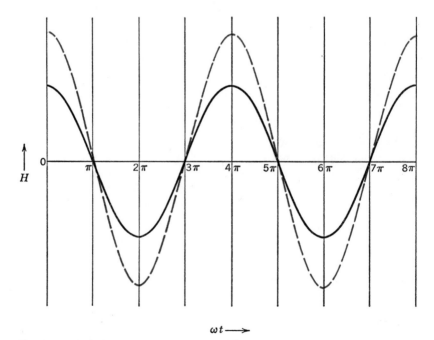

Fig. A-2.   Variation of H_x (red, — — — —) and field due to M_y (black, —————) as function of ωt when $\omega = \omega_0$.

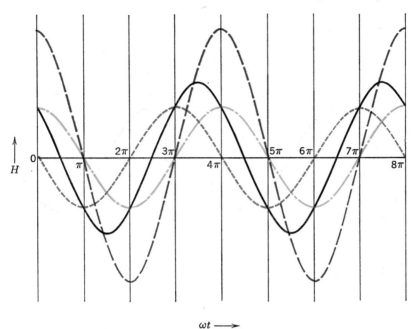

$\omega t \longrightarrow$

Fig. A-3. Variation of H_x (red, ———), field due to M_y (black ————, 45° behind H_x), component of field due to M_y in phase with H_x (green, —·—·—), and component of field due to M_y out of phase with H_x (blue, - - - -).

of phase with H_1 so that the field along the Y axis due to M_y will have its maximum value when H_x is at its maximum value. Clearly, when $\omega_0 = \omega$, the field due to M_y and the current induced in the receiver coil are a measure of the power absorbed by the nuclei, u being zero.

Matters are not so simple when $\omega \neq \omega_0$ even when the steady-state condition applies. Now the vector M_{xy} leads H_1 by 0 to 180°, depending on the magnitude of $\omega_0 - \omega$. Suppose $\omega_0 - \omega$ has values such that M_{xy} leads H_1 by 45° (Fig. A-3) or by 135° (Fig. A-4). In these circumstances, the field due to M_y lags behind or leads H_x by 45° compared with the case where $\omega_0 = \omega$. Since the components of M_y which are in phase and 90° out of phase with H_x are of particular interest, these are also plotted in Figs. A-3 and A-4.

The experimental problem in determining nuclear resonance absorption is to measure the component of the field due to M_y, which is in phase with H_x, since this corresponds to v (absorption or v mode) without interference from the component of the field due to M_y, which is out of phase with H_x and corresponds to u (dispersion or u mode). This is easily achieved by permitting some of the field H_x to "leak" into the receiver coil. Figures A-5 and A-6 show how the fields of the in-phase

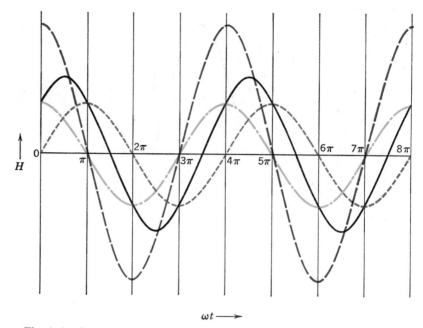

$\omega t \longrightarrow$

Fig. A-4.   Same as Fig. A-3 except now the field due to M_y leads H_x by 45°.

and out-of-phase components of magnetization combine with H_x when $\omega_0 - \omega$ is such that M_y vector is 45° ahead of H_x.

It will be noted that if the H_x leakage to the receiver coil is a bit larger than the maximum values of the field in the Y direction due to M_y, then the in-phase component of Y magnetization acts to increase the amplitude of the receiver signal without causing any phase shift. On the other hand, the sum of the H_x leakage and the out-of-phase field produced by the Y magnetization produces little increase in amplitude but does cause a phase shift (Fig. A-6). By the device of purposely introducing H_x leakage to the receiver coil, we can make the variations in signal amplitude over and above the leakage correspond to the in-phase component of M_y and hence be related to v, the measure of absorption of rf energy.

Similarly, if we arrange to leak an H_y component, the part of the field due to M_y which is out of phase with H_x is seen as amplitude modulation while the in-phase M_y primarily results in a phase shift. Consequently, it is possible to display either the absorption or dispersion modes as amplitude modulation by choosing the proper phase and magnitude of the leakage signal. The absorption mode gives a symmetrical peak centered at $\omega_0 - \omega = 0$, while the dispersion mode curve goes through

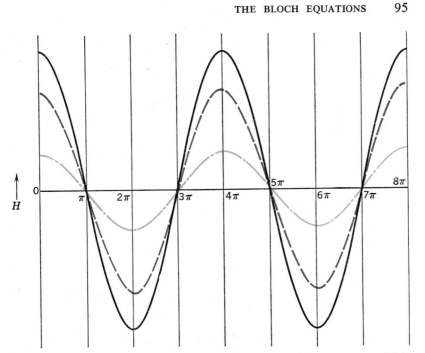

Fig. A-5. Resultant (black, ————) of addition of in-phase component of field due to M_y (green, —·—·—) to H_x leakage field (red, ———).

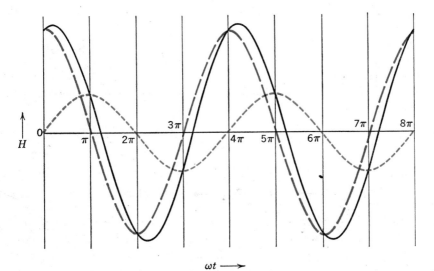

$\omega t \longrightarrow$

Fig. A-6. Resultant (black, ————) of addition of out-of-phase component of field due to M_y (blue, - - - -) to H_x leakage field (red, ———).

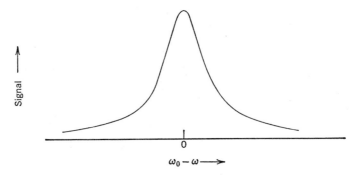

Fig. A-7.   Absorption (v)-mode signal curve.

zero at $\omega_0 - \omega = 0$ (see Figs. A-7 and A-8). The behavior of the dispersion mode curve can be clarified by inspection of Figs. A-3, A-4, and A-5, which show that the out-of-phase field component due to M_y is zero when $\omega_0 = \omega$ and will be in phase with (adding to) or 180° out of phase with (subtracting from) an H_y leakage signal when $\omega_0 \neq \omega$.

Alternatively, if one uses an rf detector which is sensitive to phase shift instead of amplitude modulation, either absorption or dispersion can be suitably measured by the appropriate choice of leakage component. The advantage of a phase-sensitive detector is that it is less influenced by variations in the oscillator output than an amplitude-sensitive detector is and as a consequence gives less base-line drift.

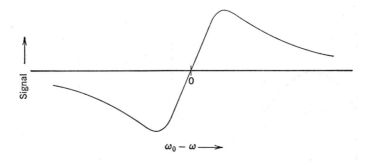

Fig. A-8.   Dispersion (u)-mode signal curve.

The magnitude of the absorption-mode a-c signal S induced in the receiver coil under slow-passage conditions can be partially expressed by the following general equation in terms of some variables of practical interest:

$$S = \text{const } N\left(\frac{I+1}{I}\right)\left(\frac{\mu^2 H_0^2}{3kT}\right)\left(\frac{\gamma^2 H_1 T_2}{1 + T_2^2(\omega_0 - \omega)^2 + \gamma^2 H_1^2 T_1 T_2}\right)$$

where N = number of nuclei in the active volume of the receiver coil
I = nuclear spin
μ = nuclear magnetic moment
k = Boltzmann's constant
T = absolute temperature

The signal strength decreases with temperature because thermal agitation opposes the lining up of the nuclei in the field direction. Increasing temperature also gives increasing electronic noise so that the signal-to-noise ratio becomes less favorable with increasing temperature even more rapidly than the signal strength itself. It will be noted that small values of H_1, such that $\gamma^2 H_1^2 T_1 T_2 \ll 1$, lead to a signal proportional to $H_1 T_2$ at the peak of the absorption curve where $\omega_0 = \omega$.

$$S = \text{const } H_1 T_2 \qquad (\text{at } \omega_0 = \omega)$$

In these circumstances $M_0 \sim M_z$, which means that the nuclear magnets are practically at thermal equilibrium with their surroundings. The signal amplitude is determined by T_2, but it is easy to show that the area under the resonance curve is independent of T_2. Furthermore, if we define the resonance line width δv as the width of the absorption curve

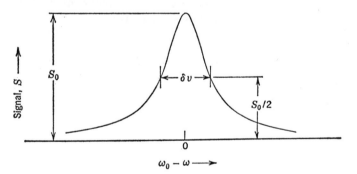

Fig. A-9. Parameter δv as width of signal curve at half-maximum intensity.

at half-maximum amplitude $S_0/2$ on a plot of signal vs. $\omega_0 - \omega$ (see Fig. A-9), then we can show that $\delta v = 2/T_2$ as follows:

$$S = \text{const } \frac{T_2}{1 + (\omega_0 - \omega)^2 T_2^2}$$

$$S_0 = \text{const } (T_2) \qquad \text{when } \omega_0 = \omega$$

$$\frac{S_0}{2} = \text{const}\,\frac{T_2}{2} = \text{const}\,\frac{T_2}{1 + (\delta v/2)^2 T_2{}^2}$$

$$T_2 = \frac{2}{\delta v}$$

As explained earlier, T_2 may be largely determined by magnetic field inhomogeneities for nonviscous liquids (pages 13 and 30).

When H_1 is large, the term $\gamma^2 H_1{}^2 T_1 T_2$ may well dominate in the denominator of the equation for signal amplitude, and in these circumstances we have

$$S = \text{const}\,\frac{1}{H_1 T_1}$$

The nuclei are then said to be "saturated," and power input is limited by the ability of longitudinal relaxation to transfer energy from the nuclei to their surroundings. Resonance signals with nuclei of low natural abundance such as deuterium in ordinary water may often be increased at large H_1 values by reducing T_1 with the aid of added paramagnetic ions such as Mn^{2+}. With many liquids, transverse relaxation is often so slow that no steady-state proton signal can be obtained without essentially complete saturation. For example, with water, T_1 and T_2 are about 4 sec, so that $\gamma^2 H_1{}^2 T_1 T_2$ is about unity when H_1 has the small value of 0.06 milligauss. It is impractical to reduce H_1 indefinitely to avoid saturation under steady-state conditions because the signal amplitude is proportional to H_1. To minimize saturation effects, the spectra of water and organic liquids are customarily run at low H_1 values under non-steady-state conditions. Such arrangements do minimize saturation but lead to signal amplitudes which are functions of the nuclear relaxation times.[2]

[2] R. B. Williams, *Ann. N.Y. Acad. Sci.,* **70,** 890 (1958).

APPENDIX B

Bibliography

The following references are in addition to those cited earlier and are mostly to general rather than specialized material.

1. *Varian Instrument Division Tech. Inform. Bull. Vol.* 1–3, Varian Associates, Palo Alto, Calif.
2. E. R. Andrew, "Nuclear Magnetic Resonance," Cambridge University Press, New York, 1955.
3. "Microwave and Radiofrequency Spectroscopy," *Discussions Faraday Soc.,* **19**, 187 (1955).
4. J. E. Wertz, *Chem. Revs.,* **55**, 829 (1955).
5. G. E. Pake, *Am. J. Phys.,* **18**, 438, 473 (1950).
6. H. M. McConnell, *Ann. Rev. Phys. Chem.,* **8**, 105 (1957).
7. C. A. Hutchison, Jr., *Ann. Rev. Phys. Chem.,* **7**, 359 (1956).
8. J. N. Shoolery and H. E. Weaver, *Ann. Rev. Phys. Chem.,* **6**, 433 (1955).
9. H. S. Gutowsky, *Ann. Rev. Phys. Chem.,* **5**, 333 (1954).
10. H. L. Richter, *J. Chem. Educ.,* **34**, 618 (1957).
11. J. A. S. Smith, *Quart. Revs. (London),* **7**, 279 (1953).
12. J. N. Shoolery, *Svensk Kem. Tidskr.,* **69**, 185 (1957).
13. J. R. Zimmerman and M. R. Foster, *J. Phys. Chem.,* **61**, 282 (1957) (standardization of spectra).
14. C. M. Huggins, G. C. Pimentel, and J. N. Shoolery, *J. Chem. Phys.,* **23**, 1244 (1955); *J. Phys. Chem.,* **60**, 1311 (1956) (molecular association).
15. "Nuclear Magnetic Resonance," *Ann. N.Y. Acad. Sci.,* **70**, 763 (1957).
16. N. F. Chamberlain, "A Catalog of Nuclear Magnetic Resonance Spectra of Hydrogen in Hydrocarbons and Their Derivatives." Available from the Research and Development Division, Humble Oil and Refining Company, Baytown, Tex.
17. J. N. Shoolery and B. Crawford, Jr., *J. Mol. Spectroscopy,* **1**, 270 (1957) (hindered rotation).

APPENDIX C

Problems

The following NMR absorption curves are given to provide practice in the interpretation of spectra. Each of the curves is for a single pure substance or solution thereof at 40 Mc using water as the reference substance. It should be possible to deduce a reasonable structure for each unknown from its molecular formula and chemical shifts, spin-spin splittings, and signal intensities as gleaned from the NMR spectra. A pair of dividers will probably be found useful in analyzing spin-spin splittings.

It must be remembered that signal heights and areas do not always have the theoretical ratios (cf. Chaps. 2 to 6 and Appendix A). Furthermore, the effects of possible exchange processes must be taken into account as discussed in Chap. 4.

C_2H_4O

-186   +144

C₄H₁₁N

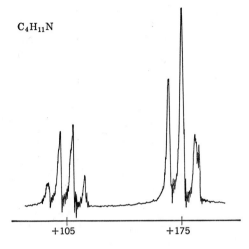

C₂H₃F₃O

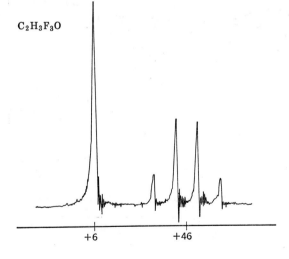

$C_{14}H_{22}O_4$

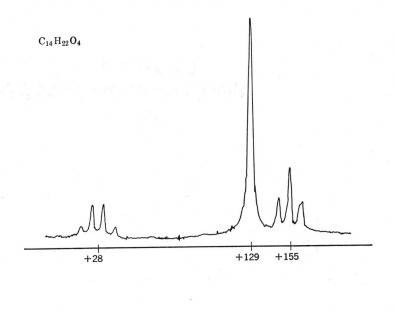

+28   +129   +155

$C_3H_5O_2Cl$

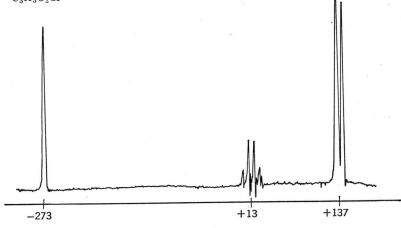

−273   +13   +137

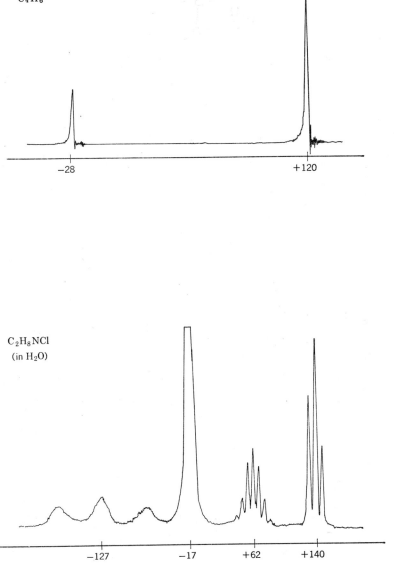

C_4H_6

-28 $+120$

C_2H_8NCl
(in H_2O)

-127 -17 $+62$ $+140$

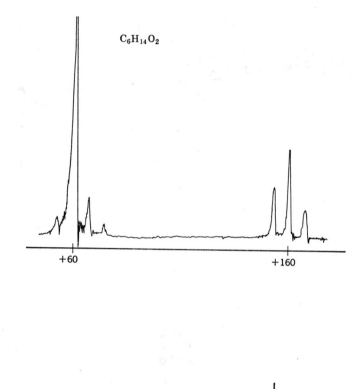

$C_6H_{14}O_2$

+60   +160

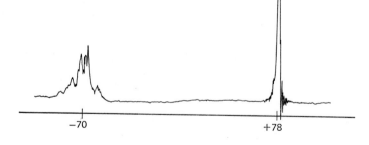

C_7H_8O

−70   +78

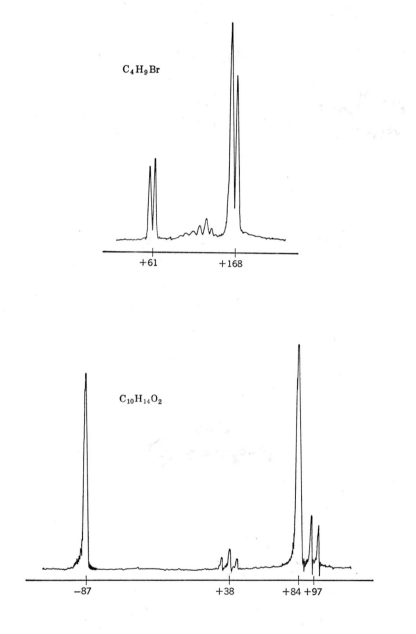

$C_6H_{12}O_2$

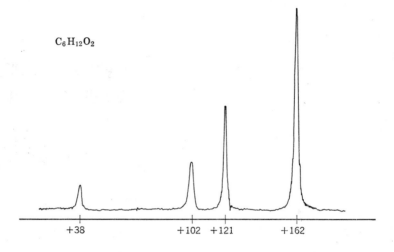

+38   +102 +121   +162

C_6H_8

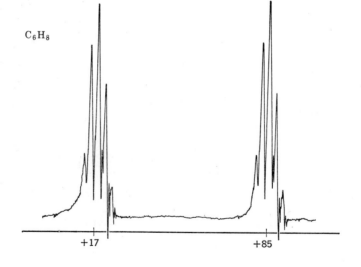

+17   +85

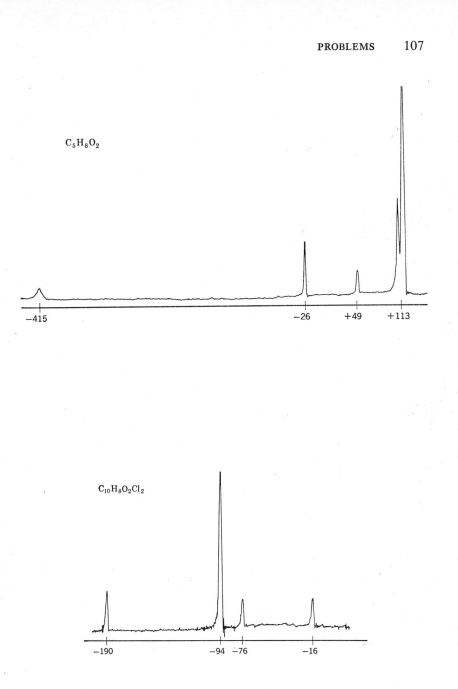

$C_5H_8O_2$

−415   −26   +49   +113

$C_{10}H_8O_2Cl_2$

−190   −94 −76   −16

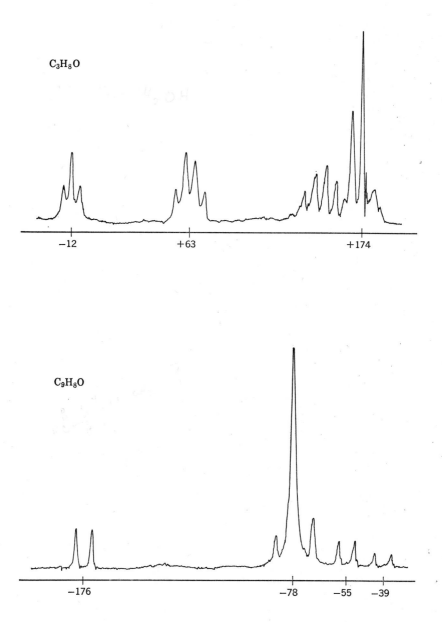

$C_5H_8O_2$

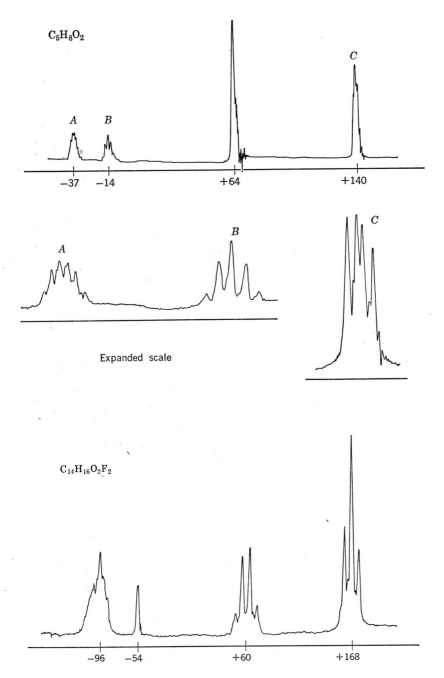

Expanded scale

$C_{14}H_{16}O_2F_2$

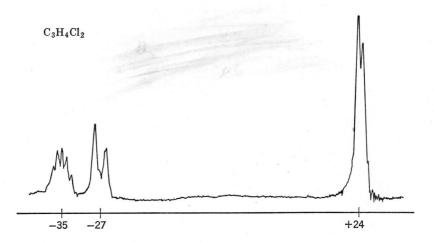

C₃H₄Cl₂

Name Index

Aldrich, P., 39, 49
Allred, A. L., 24, 25, 26
Anderson, W. A., 87
Andrew, E. R., 99
Arnold, J. T., 22

Bak, B., 86
Baker, E. B., 2
Bernstein, H. J., 55
Bloch, F., 1, 3, 88, 90, 91
Boltzmann, L., 9, 92
Bothner-By, A. A., 24, 29
Bottini, A. T., 34, 75
Brenner, G., 39, 49
Burd, L. W., 2

Caserio, M. C., 36, 40
Chamberlain, N. F., 24, 99
Cohen, A. D., 23
Corio, P. L., 29
Crawford, B. L., Jr., 99

Dailey, B. P., 26, 29

Ettlinger, M. G., 33, 35

Feist, F., 33, 34, 35
Fessenden, R. W., 29
Foster, M. R., 99
Fraenkel, G., 70
Fujiwara, S., 76

Glick, R. E., 24
Goss, F. R., 33
Grunwald, E., 79
Gutowsky, H. S., 23, 28, 29, 46, 55, 62,
    63, 76, 99

Hammett, L. P., 27, 28, 29
Hansen, W. W., 1, 3
Henriques, F. C., 74, 75
Holder, B. E., 25
Holm, C. H., 26, 63
Huggins, C. M., 99
Huggins, M. L., 26, 27
Hutchinson, C. A., 99

Ikeda, C. K., 40
Ingold, C. K., 33

Johnson, W. S., 36, 37
Jones, R., 86

Kennedy, F., 35
Kincaid, J. F., 74, 75
Kitahara, Y., 36
Klein, M. P., 25

LaForce, R. C., 25
Lauterbur, P. C., 26
Levin, S. H., 39, 49
Loewenstein, A., 79
Looney, C. E., 40

McCall, D. W., 28, 46
McConnell, H. M., 57, 99
McGarvey, B. R., 28
McLean, A. D., 57
Meiboom, S., 79
Meyer, K., 68
Meyer, L. H., 23, 28
Muetterties, E. L., 56

Nair, P. M., 58, 71
Nederbrogt, G. W., 18
Niemann, C., 70

Ogg, R. A., Jr., 76, 77

Packard, M. E., 1, 3, 22
Pake, G. E., 99
Phillips, W. D., 23, 40, 56, 69, 70, 71
Pimentel, G. C., 99
Pople, J. A., 55, 60
Pound, R. V., 1
Purcell, E. M., 1

Reid, C., 23
Reilly, C. A., 18, 57
Richter, H. L., 99
Roberts, J. D., 34, 36, 46, 58, 71, 75,
    78, 80
Rochow, E. G., 24, 25, 26
Rogers, M. T., 39

Saika, A., 23, 62
Schaeffer, R., 86
Schneider, W. G., 55
Sharts, C. M., 46

Shoolery, J. N., 26, 39, 54, 70, 84, 86, 99
Silversmith, E. F., 36
Slichter, C. P., 46
Smith, J. A. S., 99
Strombotne, R. L., 18

Taft, R. W., Jr., 29
Thorpe, J. F., 33, 35
Tolbert, B. M., 25
Torrey, H. C., 1

van Tamelen, E. E., 39, 40, 49

Waugh, J. S., 29
Weaver, H. E., 25, 99
Weinberg, I., 64
Wertz, J. E., 99
Williams, G. A., III, 86
Williams, R. B., 98
Wolinsky, J., 39, 49

Zimmerman, J. R., 64, 99

Subject Index

Abnormal diamagnetic shielding, for acetylenic protons, 30
  for aromatic protons, 29
  origin of, 29
Absorption mode, display of, 93–96
  equations for, 91
  line shape for, 96
  signal-strength equation for, 96
Acetic acid exchange with water, 61–62
Acetoacetic ester and enol, 67–68
Acetylene, abnormal diamagnetic shielding in, 30
  proton chemical shift of, 24
Alcohols, chemical shifts in, 48–51
  effect of paramagnetic salts on, 40–41
  spin-spin splitting in, 48–49
Aldehydes, proton chemical shift of, 24
Aliphatic alcohols, spin-spin coupling with, 48–49
Allene, proton-proton couplings in, 46, 54
Amides, mode of protonation, 70–71
  rotation about bonds, 69–70
Ammonia, NMR spectrum, 77
  proton exchange in, 76–77
Ammonium nitrate, NMR spectrum, 77–78
  proton exchange with water, 77–78
Analysis, quantitative, 30, 40
  of acetic acid–water systems, 62
  illustrative, of reaction product, 40
  of keto-enol equilibrium, 68
  of rapidly exchanging systems, 62
  of rotational isomer populations, 71–73
  (*See also* Structure analysis)
Areas (*see* Signal peak areas)
Aromatic compounds, abnormal diamagnetic shielding in, 29
  ^{19}F δ values, 28
  proton δ values, 29
Aromatic rings, proton-proton couplings through, 54
Asymmetry, molecular, and spin-spin splitting, 58–60
Audio-oscillator beat method for measurement of line spacings, 22

Base catalysis, of amine-proton exchange, 80–81, 84
  of ammonia proton exchange, 76–77
  of ethyl acetoacetate exchange, 67–68
Bloch equations, derivation of, 88–91
Boron hydrides, double resonance with, 86
Bromine, quadrupole relaxation with, 84–85
Bromoallene, proton-proton couplings in, 46, 54
Bulk diamagnetic susceptibility and solvent effects, 24
t-Butyl alcohol, NMR spectrum, 51

^{12}C, ^{13}C (*see* Carbon)
Carbon, ^{12}C, nuclear properties of, 6
  ^{13}C, δ values for, 26
  ease of NMR detection, 18
  nuclear properties of, 6, 18
  nuclear relaxation of, 12
Chemical exchange, acetic acid and water, 61–62
  in alcohols, 49, 64–66
  ammonia and water, 76–77
  ammonium ion and water, 77–78
  and chemical shift, 63–64
  determination of rates of, 61–68, 76–79
  effect on quadrupole-broadened lines, 84–86
  in ethanol-water, 64–66
  Feist's acid and water, 34–35
  and line shapes, 64–65
  methylammonium ion and water, 78–79
  of OH and effect on alcohol spectra, 49
  proton, in ammonia and ammonium ions, 76–79
  in pyrrole, 84
  pyrrolidine hydrochloride and water, 80–81
  and spin-spin splitting, 65–66
Chemical shift, and abnormal diamagnetic shielding, 29–30
  accentuation by paramagnetic salts, 40–41

Chemical shift, of acetylene protons, 24, 30
  of aldehyde protons, 24
  aromatic protons, 29
  bulk diamagnetic susceptibility effects on, 22, 24
  δ values, definition of, 21
    ^{14}N, 25
    ^{17}O, 25
  protons, 23
  dependence on field strength, 21
  and diamagnetic shielding, 21
  effect of paramagnetic salts on, 40–41
  and electronegativity, 26–27
  and ethanol spectrum, 20
  internal reference standards for, 21, 24
  measurement of, 21
  methylene protons of 1,4-decamethylenebenzene, 29
  and paramagnetic effect, 21
  reference standards for, 21, 24
  relation of, to exchange processes, 63–64
    to Hammett equation, 27–29
  solvent effects on, 21–24
  solvent effects on methyl resonances, 24–25
  and spin-spin splitting, 55–56
  of sulfonic acid protons, 24
  temperature effects on, 22–23
  and torsional vibrations, 23
Chlorine, quadrupole relaxation with, 84–85
  ^{35}Cl, nuclear properties, 7
Chlorine trifluoride, spin-spin splitting in, 56
4-Chloro-3-phenyl-3-butenoic acid, NMR proof of structure, 36
2-Chloro-3-phenylcyclobutenone, acid from ring-opening of, 36
Conformations, analysis of, by NMR, 71–74
  different, H-H coupling constants for, 54
  proton resonances in, 39
Coupling constants, for ethyl group, 46
  factors determining, 46
  in H-D crystal, 45
  proton-fluorine, in cyclobutenes, 46
  in fluorobenzene, 86
  proton-proton, in aliphatic compounds, 53, 54
    in allene, 46, 54
    through aromatic rings, 54, 86
    in cyclobutene, 54
    as function of conformation, 54
    in photosantonic acid, 53
    through quinoid rings, 54
    in unsaturated compounds, 46, 54
  in relation to internuclear separations, 46

Coupling constants, in styrene oxide, 48
  in tumbling molecules, 45–46
Crossed-coil spectrometer (see Spectrometer)
Cyclic molecules, spin-spin splittings in, 57
Cyclobutene, proton signal peak areas of, 32
  spin-spin splitting in, 54
  substituted, H-F splittings, 46
Cyclopentanone, NMR spectrum, 57

1,4-Decamethylenebenzene, methylene resonances in, 29
δ values (see Chemical shift)
Deuterated solvents, 34
Deuterium, double resonance with, 86
  ease of NMR detection, 18–19, 98
  effect on NMR spectrum when substituted for proton, 20, 86
  nuclear properties, 7, 18
  use in determination of spin-spin splittings, 86
Diamagnetic shielding, abnormal, with unsaturated compounds, 29–30
  and chemical shift, 21
1,2-Dibromo-2-methylpropane, lack of spin-spin splitting in, 59–60
  NMR spectrum, 58
  rotational conformations, 59–60
1,1-Difluoro-1,2-dibromo-2,3-dichloroethane, ^{19}F spectrum of, temperature effects on, 71–73
  rotational conformations, 71–73
1,1-Difluoroethylene, NMR spectrum, 57–58
  spin-spin splitting in, 57–58
1,1-Difluoro-1,2,2-tribromo-2-phenylethane, NMR spectrum at −80°, 72
  rotational conformations, 72–73
Dimethylformamide, mode of protonation, 70–71
  NMR spectrum, 69
  rotation about amide bond, 69–70
Dipole-dipole interaction, intramolecular, 45
Dispersion mode, display of, 93–96
  equations for, as u, 91–92
  line shape for, 96
Double resonance, 84–85, 86–87
  and boron hydrides, 86
  with deuterium, 86
  with deuterofluorobenzenes, 86
  with ^{14}N, 84
  and pyrrole, 84
  technique of, 84

Electric quadrupole, 7
  (See also Nuclear relaxation)
Electronegativity, calculation from δ values, 26
  relation to δ values, 26–27

Equivalent nuclei, spin-spin splitting and, 55–58
Ethanes, restricted rotation in, 71–74
  rotational conformations of, 58–60
Ethanol, exchange with water, 64–66
  hydroxyl resonance, change with temperature and solvent, 23
  spectrum of, high-resolution, 42, 50
    low-resolution, 20
  signal areas in, 20
  and water mixtures, 64–66
Ethyl acetate, effect of spinning on NMR spectrum of, 31
Ethyl acetoacetate, and exchange with enol form, 67–68
  NMR spectrum, 67
N-Ethylallenimine, inversion frequency, 75–76
  NMR spectrum, 76
Ethylenimines, inversion frequencies, 74–76
N-Ethylethylenimine, inversion frequency, 3, 74
  NMR spectrum, 2
  effect of temperature on, 74–75
Ethyl group, chemical shifts of, 26–27
  coupling constants for, 46
  in N-ethylethylenimine, 2
  spin-spin splitting in, 42–43, 46–47, 55
Exchange (see Chemical exchange; Inversion; Rotation)

^{19}F (see Fluorine)
Feist's acid, proof of structure by NMR, 33–35
  proton exchange of, 35
Fluorine, ^{19}F, ease of NMR detection, 18–19
  nuclear properties, 6, 18
  (See also Chemical shift; Coupling constants; Spin-spin splitting)
Fluorobenzene, deuterated, NMR spectra, 86–87
  spin-spin splitting in, 86
  substituted, δ values for, 28
Free rotation effect on NMR spectra, 59–60, 71–74

Gyromagnetic ratio (see Nuclear precession)

^{2}H (see Deuterium)
^{1}H (see Proton)
Halogens, quadrupole relaxation with, 84–85
Hammett equation, 27–28
  and ^{19}F δ values, 28
  and proton δ values, 29
Hydrogen-bonding, influence on NMR spectra, 23, 40
  and inversion of imines, 76

Hydrogen-bonding, solvent effects on, 23, 40
  temperature effects on, 23
Hydrogen deuteride, spin-spin splitting in, 43–46
Hydroxyl resonance, of acetic acid–water mixtures, 61–62
  change with hydrogen-bonding, 23, 40
  of ethanol-water mixtures, 64–66

Imines, cyclic, inversion frequencies of, 74–76
Internal standards, 21–22, 24
Inversion, of cyclic imines, 74–76
  hydrogen bonding and, 76
  resonance and, 75
Iodine, quadrupole relaxation with, 84–85
Isopropyl alcohol, NMR spectrum, 49, 51
  spin-spin splitting in, 49

J (see Coupling constants; Spin-spin splitting)

Keto-enol equilibria, 67–68

Leakage adjustments, NMR probe, 93–96
Line shapes, and exchange rates, 63–64
  and quadrupole broadening, 80–86
Line spacings, measurement, 21–22
Line width, equation for, 97
  influence of relaxation times on, 30, 97
  natural, 30
Longitudinal relaxation (see Nuclear relaxation)

Magnet (see Spectrometer)
Magnetic field, H_0, effect on signal strength, 96
  homogeneity of (see Spectrometer)
Magnetic moment, nuclear, 6, 7
Magnetic quantum numbers, nuclear, 7–9
Magnetic susceptibility effects, 22, 24
Magnetogyric ratio, 10
Methylammonium chloride, exchange with water, 78–79
  NMR spectrum, 78
  quadrupole broadening with, 78, 80
Methyl 2,3-dibromo-2-methylpropionate, NMR spectrum, 58–59
  rotational conformations, 59
  spin-spin splitting in, 58–59
Methylenecyclopropane-1,2-dicarboxylic acid, 33–35
Methyl groups, δ values of, 25
  solvent effects on, 24–25
Methyl phenyldimethylcarbinol ether, NMR spectrum, 40

α-Methylstyrene, NMR spectrum, 40
Molecular asymmetry, detection by NMR of, 59–60
and spin-spin splitting, 58–60
Molecular tumbling, effect of, on quadrupole broadening, 82
on spin-spin splitting, 45–46

^{14}N, ^{15}N (see Nitrogen)
Natural line width, 30
Nitrogen, H-N proton resonances, 76–81, 83–86
^{14}N, δ values, 25
ease of NMR detection, 18
nuclear properties, 7, 18
quadrupole relaxation, 80–86
^{15}N, ease of NMR detection, 18
nuclear properties, 6, 18
(See also Amides; Ammonia; Ammonium nitrate)
2-Nitro-2-methyl-1,3-propanediol, rotational conformations, 60
spin-spin splitting in, 60
Nuclear charge distributions, 6–7
Nuclear induction spectrometer (see Spectrometer)
Nuclear magnetic moment, 6, 7
Nuclear magnetic properties, 5–10, 18
Nuclear magnetic quantum numbers, possible values, 7–8
distribution between, 8–9
Nuclear magnetization, 8–9
changes, in NMR absorption, 88–92
(See also Nuclear relaxation; Nuclear resonance absorption)
effect of temperature on, 8–9
Nuclear precession, 10
frequencies, 10, 18
gyromagnetic ratio, 10
magnetogyric ratio, 10
Nuclear quadrupole, 7
(See also Nuclear relaxation)
Nuclear quadrupole moment, 5–7
Nuclear quadrupole relaxation (see Nuclear relaxation)
Nuclear relaxation, ^{13}C rates, 12
characteristic times of, 12–14
effect on, of motion of magnetic nuclei, 11
of paramagnetic substances, 12, 98
of temperature, 11, 14
of viscosity, 11, 14
effects on signal strength, 17, 30–31, 96–98
energy transfer in, 9–10
longitudinal, 12
effect on signal strengths, 30–31, 96–97
mechanisms for, 10–14, 81–83
quadrupole effects, 80–86
with halogen nuclei, 84–85
mechanism of, 81–83

Nuclear relaxation, quadrupole effects, with ^{14}N, 80–86
temperature effects on, 81–84
T_1 as longitudinal relaxation time, 12
T_2 as transverse relaxation time, 13
transverse, 13
effect of, on line widths, 30, 97
on signal strengths, 30–31, 96–97
effect on, of field inhomogeneities, 13
of spin-spin collisions, 14
of structure, 18
of viscosity, 13–14
measurement of rate, 18
relaxation wiggles and, 17–18
T_2, as line-width parameter, 97
Nuclear resonance absorption, basic apparatus for, 1
(See also Spectrometer)
Bloch theory, 88–98
display of, 93–96
equations for, as v, 91
line shape for, 96
mechanism, 16–17
signal-strength equation for, 96
Nuclear resonance dispersion, display of, 93–96
equations for, as u, 91–92
line shape for, 96
Nuclear spin, 5
relation to magnetic quantum numbers, 8
values of, 18
Nuclear spin decoupling (see Double resonance)

^{16}O, ^{17}O (see Oxygen)
Oxygen, ^{16}O, nuclear properties, 6
^{17}O, chemical-shift values, 25
ease of NMR detection, 18
nuclear properties, 7, 18

^{31}P (see Phosphorus)
Paramagnetic effects on chemical shift, 21, 40–41
Paramagnetic ions, effect of, on chemical shift, 40–41
on signal strength, 98
Peak areas (see Signal peak areas)
Phase-memory time, 13
(See also Nuclear relaxation)
Phase-sensitive detector, 96
Phenyldimethylcarbinol, NMR spectrum, 40
Phosphorus, ^{31}P, ease of NMR detection, 18
nuclear properties, 6, 18
Photosantonic acid, structure proof of, 39, 49, 52–53
Precession (see Nuclear precession)
n-Propyl alcohol, NMR spectrum, 50
Proton-deuteron exchange, Feist's acid, 35

Protons, chemical exchanges of, 34–35, 61–68, 76–81, 84
  δ values for 23, 29
  and σ constants, 29
  double resonance with, 86–87
  ease of NMR detection, 18–19
  exchange, between acetic acid–water, 61–62
    between ethanol-water, 64–66
    between keto-enol forms, 67–68
  nuclear properties, 6, 18
  (See also Chemical shift; Coupling constants; Spin-spin splitting)
Pyrrole, quadrupole broadening and, 83–84
  NMR spectrum, 83
  proton exchange in, 84
Pyrrolidine hydrochloride, exchange with water, 80–81
  NMR spectrum, 81
  quadrupole broadening with, 80–83

Quadrupole, electric, 7
  (See also Nuclear relaxation)
Quadrupole broadening, mechanism, 81–82
  temperature effects on, 81–84
Quadrupole-induced relaxation, 80–86
  (See also Nuclear relaxation)
Quadrupole moment, nuclear, 5–7
Quantitative analysis (see Analysis)
Quinones, proton-proton couplings in, 54

Rate constants, determination by NMR, 63–66
Reaction kinetics, determination by NMR, 61–78
Reference standards, 21, 24
  (See also Chemical shift)
Relaxation (see Nuclear relaxation)
Relaxation wiggles, 17
  effect of T_2 on, 17, 18
Restricted rotation, in amides, 69–70
  effect on NMR spectra, 59–60, 69–74
  in nitrites, N-nitrosoamines, oximes, 71
  in substituted ethanes, 71–74
Rf detector, 1, 3, 15–16
Rf oscillator (see Spectrometer)
Rotating field, H_1, equations for, 88
Rotating-field vector, in nuclear relaxation, 11
  rf oscillator, 15–16, 88
Rotation, free, effect on NMR spectra, 59–60, 71–74
  restricted, effect on NMR spectra, 59–60, 71–74

Sample, spinning, and line widths, 30
  thermostated apparatus for, 30, 32
Sample preparation, illustrative, 33–34

Saturation effects, 17, 30–31, 98
Second-order spin-spin splitting, 42, 56
Sensitivities to detection of NMR signals, nuclear properties and, 18, 19, 96
  isotope abundances and, 19
Sidebands produced by audio oscillator, 22
σ constants, Hammett equation, 27–29
Signal peak areas, 30–32
  abnormal cyclobutene proton, 32
  effect of temperature on, 96–97
  ethanol spectrum, 20
  as function, of H_1, 30–32, 98
    of relaxation times, 30–32, 97–98
  and spin-spin splitting, 55–56
  use of, in analysis, 30–32
  in structure proofs, 32, 34, 36
Signal strength, as function, of H_0, 96
  of H_1, 30–31, 96–98
  paramagnetic ions and, 98
  saturation effects on, 98
  for various nuclei, 18–19
Slow-passage conditions, 30, 91–98
Solids, inapplicability of, to high-resolution NMR, 33
Solvent effects on methyl resonances, 24–25
Solvents, deuterated, 34
  effects on chemical shifts, 21–25
  for NMR work, 33–34
  nonhydrogenous, 34
Spectrometer, NMR, arrangement of coils in, 4–5, 14–15
  block diagrams, 2–5
  crossed-coil apparatus, 3–5, 14–15
  magnet for, 1, 3
    field values, 19
    homogeneity of field, 13, 42
  principles of operation, 1–5, 14–17
  rf detector in, 1, 3, 15–16
  rf oscillator in, 1, 3, 15–16
    frequencies for, 19
  sweep generator for, 3, 15
Spin (see Nuclear spin)
Spin decoupling (see Double resonance)
Spin-spin collisions, 14
Spin-spin splitting, averaged through rotation, 59–60
  and chemical exchange, 65–66, 76–77, 80–81, 84
  and chemical shift, 55–56
  chlorine trifluoride, 56
  in cyclic molecules, 57
  in cyclobutene, 54
  1,1-difluoroethylene, 57–58
  with equivalent nuclei, 55–58
  in ethanol, 42, 46–48, 64–66
  fluorine-proton, 46, 57–58, 86
  in fluorobenzene, 86
  in "frozen-in" rotational isomers, 71–74

Spin-spin splitting, invariance with field strength, 43, 45
  in methyl 2,3-dibromo-2-methylpropionate, 58–59
  and molecular asymmetry, 58–60
  in 2-nitro-2-methyl-1,3-propanediol, 60
  of nuclei of different kinds, 56
  in photosantonic acid, 52–53
  proton-deuteron, 86
  proton-^{14}N, 77–81
  and quadrupole relaxation, 81–86
  and rotational conformations, 54, 58–60, 71–74
  second-order, 56
    in ethanol, 42
  and signal peak areas, 55–56
  simplification by double resonance, 86–87
  in single crystal, 43–45
  in structure determination of photosantonic acid, 52–53
  in styrene oxide, 48
  with tumbling molecules, 45–46
  (See also Coupling constants)
Spin temperature, nonequilibrium, 11
Spinner, sample, thermostated, 30, 32
  use to reduce line widths, 30
Splitting (see Spin-spin splitting)
Standards, internal, 21–22, 24
  reference, 21, 24
Steroids, NMR spectra, 39
  proof of structure of synthetic intermediate to, 36–38
Structure analysis, 4-chloro-3-phenyl-3-butenoic acid, 36
  through double resonance, 86–87
  N-ethylethylenimine, 2, 74–75
  Feist's acid, 33–35
  hydrogen conformations in steroids, 39
  photosantonic acid, 39–40, 49, 52–53
  and spin-spin splitting, 46–55, 58–60
  tetracyclic ketol and dehydration product, 36–37
Styrene oxide, spin-spin splitting in, 48
Sulfonic acid, proton chemical shift of, 24
Sulfur, ^{33}S, nuclear properties, 7
Sweep generator (see Spectrometer)
Sweep rate effect on signal, 17, 98

T_1 (see Nuclear relaxation, longitudinal)
T_2 (see Nuclear relaxation, transverse)
Temperature effects, on ethanol spectrum, 23
  on ethyl acetoacetate, 67–68
  on imine inversion, 74–76
  on proton exchanges, 78, 80–81
  on rates of rotation, amide bonds, 69–70
    single bonds, 71–73
  on signal strength, 96–97
  on 1,1,2,2-tetrafluoro-3-phenylcyclobutane spectrum, 23
  and torsional vibrations, 23
1,1,2,2-Tetrafluoro-3-phenylcyclobutane and temperature change of ^{19}F resonance, 23
Thymolhydroquinone monomethyl ether, coupling constants, 54
Torsional vibrations effect on chemical shift, 23
Transition times in NMR spectroscopy, 62–63
Transverse relaxation (see Nuclear relaxation)
Tumbling molecules, quadrupole broadening in, 82
  spin-spin splittings in, 45–46

u mode, display of, 93–96
  equations for, 91–92
  line shape for, 96
Unsaturated compounds, proton-proton couplings in, 46, 54

v mode, display of, 93–96
  equations for, 91
  line shape for, 96
  signal-strength equation for, 96
Viscosity, effect of, on line width, 33
  on T_1 and T_2, 11–14

Water exchange, with acetic acid, 61–62
  with ammonia, 77
  with ammonium ion, 77–78
  with ethanol, 64–66
  with pyrrolidine hydrochloride, 80–81
Water relaxation times, 98
Wiggles, relaxation, 17